WITHDRAWN-DOVER

D1167546

THE FIELD GUIDE TO
UFOs

DATE DUE			
546170			
GAYLORD 234			PRINTED IN U.S.A.

STACK

1/00

Other *Field Guides*
to the Unknown

THE FIELD GUIDE TO EXTRATERRESTRIALS
by Patrick Huyghe
THE FIELD GUIDE TO BIGFOOT, YETI, AND OTHER MYSTERY PRIMATES WORLDWIDE
by Loren Coleman and Patrick Huyghe

Available in October 2000 . . .

THE FIELD GUIDE TO GHOSTS AND OTHER APPARITIONS
by Hilary Evans and Patrick Huyghe

THE FIELD GUIDE TO
UFOs

A CLASSIFICATION OF VARIOUS UNIDENTIFIED AERIAL PHENOMENA BASED ON EYEWITNESS ACCOUNTS

DENNIS STACY and PATRICK HUYGHE

Illustrated by Harry Trumbore

Quill

An Imprint of HarperCollinsPublishers

HarperCollins books may be purchased for educational, business, or sales
promotional use. For information please write: Special Markets Department,
HarperCollins Publishers Inc., 10 East 53rd Street, New York, NY 10022-5299.

FIRST EDITION

Designed by Stanley S. Drate/Folio Graphics Co., Inc.

Library of Congress Cataloging-in-Publication Data has been applied for.
ISBN 0-380-80265-1

00 01 02 03 04 RRD 10 9 8 7 6 5 4 3 2 1

*To my mom, Minnie, who instilled a lifelong interest in
the odd and unusual, and my wife, Julie, who continues
to put up with it.*
—DS

*To my parents, Alain and Gladys, who always supported
my interest in the odd and unusual, and my wife,
Carolyn, who continues to put up with it.*
—PH

CONTENTS

INTRODUCTION

AN EMBARRASSMENT OF RICHES

The late J. Allen Hynek, Air Force astronomy consultant for Project Blue Book and founder of the Center for UFO Studies that now bears his name, once referred to the sheer number of UFO reports as an "embarrassment of riches." The numbers would certainly seem to bear him out. One Gallup public opinion poll revealed that nine percent of the adult American population—equivalent to about 11 million people at the time—had seen what they thought was a UFO. Extrapolated worldwide and over time, the number of UFO witnesses from the last half century alone easily extends to the tens, if not hundreds, of millions—only a minuscule fraction of which are ever reported to the military, law enforcement officials, or civilian UFO research organizations. The most commonly reported reason for failing to make a report public is fear of ridicule from one's family, friends, neighbors, colleagues.

This inherent embarrassment of numbers includes an embarrassment of forms as well. While the general public perceives flying saucers and Unidentified Flying Objects as one and the same, the reports paint a dramatically different picture. Indeed, the classic "flying saucer"—imagine a spinning, discus-shaped object with a smaller, rounded dome or canopy in the center—is on a par with such Hollywood stereotypes as the prostitute with a heart of gold and the stolid, solitary gunslinger. In reality, so-called "daylight discs," as they are referred to by ufologists (those who study UFOs as a hobby or avocation), constitute but a small percentage of all UFOs reported. The overwhelming majority of UFO reports belong to what Hynek called "nocturnal lights," those amorphous blobs of variously colored lights seen singly or in formation against the dark background of the night.

1

Obviously, if we had had, say, 37 million reports of the same object since Kenneth Arnold's landmark 1947 sighting, we would all be more or less agreed that an invasion of advanced—and presumably extraterrestrial—technology was now well under way. But the fact of the matter is that UFOs are routinely reported in a vastly bewildering variety of shapes, forms, and behavior. It's one thing to contemplate that we're being visited on a regular, if not daily basis, by extraterrestrial visitors. But it's quite another to posit the position that planet Earth represents little more than a convenient truck stop on some intergalactic highway, a brief stopover between one edge of the Milky Way and the other for every passing vehicle of alien manufacture and its occupants.

In short, both the number and variety of shapes involved would seem to automatically argue that what is popularly regarded as the UFO phenomenon is actually several discrete phenomena. The one may be many, in other words, and almost certainly is. Both military and civilian studies of UFOs, for example, reveal that the overwhelming majority are merely misperceived mundane objects or atmospheric or astronomical phenomena, what are referred to in the vernacular as IFOs, *Identified* Flying Objects. All too often, a brilliantly scintillating and stationary Venus (or other celestial object) is still reported as a distant or nearby UFO.

Weather balloons commonly give rise to UFO reports, too, as do aircraft landing lights, mirages, advertising planes and blimps, and hoaxes of varying sorts. (An increasingly popular hoax is the small balloon with road flares attached.) Natural phenomena may be involved as UFO instigators as well, a category that could include such little understood but nonetheless recognized candidates as earthquake lights and ball lighting.

On the other hand, many UFO reports seem to be just that—reliable eyewitness accounts of a previously and as yet unidentified object or phenomenon. The cases we have collected here will, hopefully, demonstrate that point.

THE FIRST FLYING SAUCER

On June 24, 1947, pilot Kenneth Arnold of Boise, Idaho, was flying his private plane, a Callair, in the vicinity of Mount Rainier when he spotted nine distant, silvery objects traveling at a high rate of speed, sunlight glinting off their shiny surfaces. After landing in nearby Yakima, Washington, Arnold reported what he had seen. When interviewed by Associated Press reporter Bill Bequette, he compared their motion as they flew to that of "a saucer skipping over water." Bequette's article went out over the AP wire, some anonymous headline writer coined the phrase "flying saucer," and the rest, as they say, is history. A history of what is another matter entirely.

Almost overnight, flying saucers passed into the public imagination, where they have flourished ever since. Now, at the beginning of the twenty-first century, every child and adult from the Cascades to the Caucasuses knows what a flying saucer is supposed to look like. The image of a spinning, supersleek, perfectly circular spaceship from another planet is indelibly etched in our collective minds. But there is a problem with this picture. Although what Arnold saw that historical day remains unexplained—and his name remains forever synonymous with the first flying saucer—what he actually reported bore no resemblance to a classic flying disc whatsoever. (See Figure 1.) The details, in other words, had been lost in the headlines.

Arnold's own sketch, which was attached to a report made three weeks after the event and addressed to the "Commanding General, Wright Field, Dayton, Ohio," does resemble a disc when seen in side view. On the other hand, the pictured object could just as easily be described as cigar-shaped. (Indeed, had he seen the objects only from an edge-on angle, he might well have described them as such.) But Arnold also included a top view of his flying "saucer" that in no way resembles a perfect circle. The best way to describe it is as heel-shaped, with the rounded end indicating the direction of travel. The back end of this now reversed shoe heel isn't an abrupt perpendicular or indented concave, but rather a gentle, convex line connecting the two outer sides of the "heel." Arnold estimated the objects' size as less than that of a DC-4, which he could also see nearby.

Others also saw strange objects in the skies over Washington on that fateful day. A prospector named Fred Johnson observed six silent discs about twelve miles from Mount Rainier. He de-

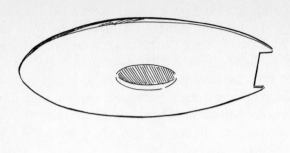

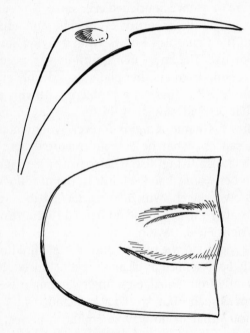

Figure 1

Top: A version of Arnold's own sketch of the side view of the objects he saw in 1947.

Middle: What Kenneth Arnold saw on June 24, 1947, according to the illustration that appeared on the cover of his book with Ray Palmer *The Coming of the Saucers* in 1952.

Bottom: A version of Arnold's own sketch of the top view of what he saw that day.

4

scribed them as "round, but with tails." Then several hours after the Arnold sighting dozens watched light blue and purple balls of light performing aerobatic maneuvers over Seattle. Flying *saucers?* Not exactly.

THE PROBLEM OF HUMAN OBSERVATION

As a species, *Homo sapiens* is indeed a marvel of millions of years of evolutionary engineering, what with our enormous, convoluted brains, color binocular vision, and other sophisticated modes of perception. But Aldous Huxley was only half right when he referred to these as the "doors of perception." He might just as well have labeled the human sensory system "shutters of perception," for we consciously perceive and partake of but a small slice of everything that is. We smell only a limited range of all odors, hear but a small segment of all sound frequencies, and see only through a limited window the entire vibrating spectrum of light.

While the truth is out there, it may not always be truthfully perceived. The hard-wired limitations alone, limitations built into our biological sensors, guarantee that. The best we can ever hope for is but a fleeting glimpse or internalized impression of reality. Put another way, humans are imperfect observers by definition; at the same time, human observations constitute the largest single body of "evidence" in favor of the UFO phenomenon. The problem is further complicated by what might be called software issues of perception, the tendency to see what we expect or are psychologically predisposed to see.

Examples of hard-wired errors of perception are literally legion. Because our eyes dart constantly (and unconsciously) about when focusing, for example, a distant pinpoint of light such as a planet or star may appear to jump back and forth in space, when in reality it remains perfectly stationary. Our eyes play other perceptual tricks as well. A bright object viewed against a dark sky inevitably looms larger than it really is. Conversely, a dark object seen in broad daylight against a bright backdrop will appear smaller than it really is.

Consider something as ordinarily familiar as the moon. A full moon low on the horizon may loom almost twice as large in the mind's eye as the same lunar disc when seen straight overhead. The difference in apparent size (which can also make an object appear closer or farther away than it actually is) in this instance is probably attributable to factors of both color and proximity to other points of reference. When low on the horizon, the moon appears more orange in color and closer in relation to buildings, water towers, trees, and other known objects of reference. Seen directly overhead, the moon is both more isolated and whiter, dwarfed by the surrounding dark spaces, and therefore perceived as more distant and smaller when compared with its near-horizon counterpart. All things being equal, however, a bright light source will be invariably interpreted as closer than a dim one, even when the two sources are at the exact same distance.

Perspective also plays havoc with perception. To take the simplest example, a commercial passenger plane seen overhead, at a 90-degree angle to the observer, would appear as a cross or plus sign. (See Figure 2.) Seen at a different angle, it might more closely resemble the letter X. Which shape is true or "truer"? The answer is that both shapes are true, depending on the position of the observer and his or her perspective to the airplane.

Similarly, it's easy to see how a classic "flying saucer" might be described as a cigar shape by one witness, an elongated oval by another, or as a perfectly round sphere by yet a third, depending on nothing more than perspective. (See Figure 3.) Again, all three shapes would be true to the original observer. Unfortunately for the ufologist trying to make sense of the phenomenon, the same object might be reported as three singular shapes, or separate UFOs, by three different observers in three locations. Obviously, it's the perspective of the observer that's changed and not the UFO itself. (But, as we shall see, UFOs have been reported to dramatically change shape on occasion, in ways that can't be attributed to a simple shift in the angle of sight—or, for that matter, easily incorporated into a single, unified UFO theory.)

Another significant factor in determining a UFO's shape is its

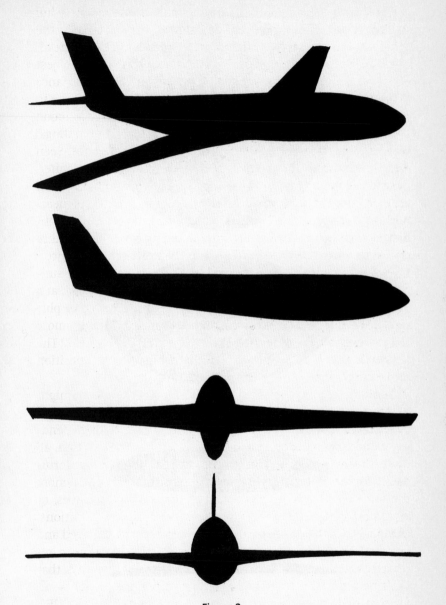

Figure 2

An airplane viewed from different angles.

Figure 3

A "flying saucer" seen from different angles.

behavior. Disc-shaped UFOs, for instance, have been reported with a bewildering variety of external appurtenances, everything from antennas, flaps, flanges, and fins, to legs, domes, round portholes, and square windows. To return to our airplane analogy, if some UFOs are indeed physical objects, then we might arguably expect their profile to change over time as well, depending on deliberate activity and intention, in the same way that a commercial jet with landing gear and flaps extended for takeoff or landing looks dramatically different than the same plane in level flight. In other words, legs, antennas, and fins, along with other "deviations" from the norm, might be merely temporary manifestations rather than fixed forms.

Apart from the issue of human perception and fallibility, there is the matter of the individual witness. As outsiders, we have no way of knowing whether a particular witness is telling the truth as best he or she perceived it, exaggerating for effect (which sometimes takes place over time), or merely fabricating a blatant hoax—for reasons both publicly admitted and left unknown. In other words, some UFO hoaxers have come forth and others haven't. Indeed, this is why investigations are conducted in the first place.

THE ARNOLD PHENOMENON

What immediately becomes clear in such an investigation is that some human observers are more imperfect than others. Kenneth Arnold, whose landmark 1947 sighting propelled UFOs into public prominence, is arguably a case in point. For starters, Arnold was a "repeater," meaning he reported UFOs on more than one occasion. Simply because an individual sees UFOs on more than one occasion shouldn't necessarily render their testimony suspect, and, in his defense, Arnold was a professional pilot who spent a considerable amount of his life in the air. On the other hand, it at least raises the question of whether such repeaters are prone to see UFOs in circumstances, or under the influence of stimuli, that the majority of us might dismiss as merely mundane.

For the record, Arnold's second sighting came in the early morning hours of July 29, 1947, shortly after he had taken off from Boise, Idaho, bound for Chehallis, Washington, a route he had flown many times. As he was descending into La Grande, Oregon, to refuel, Arnold was suddenly confronted "by a flock of what looked like ducks." He wrote: "I knew they weren't ducks because they were brassy-colored and large—at least three feet across or possibly four or five. There were a couple of dozen of them, and they were coming right at me. Eventually they swerved away—and because they had the flight characteristics of the first flying saucers, I decided to take after them. When I dived into the cluster, these things, whatever they were, soared away as if I were standing still."

In 1952, Arnold saw the saucers again, when "two of them flew under me at Mount Lassen. I got a movie of these, and one was just as solid as a Chevrolet car. But you could see the pine trees right through the other one that was following it." Arnold would come to conclude that the flying saucers represented not some sort of nuts-and-bolts spaceships, but living creatures of some kind.

By Arnold's own admission, his UFO experiences forever altered his life—as well as ours, it would seem! Because his name was prominently displayed in the papers in association with his original sighting, other people began to call and write Arnold to report similar sightings. He became an unofficial repository for such material, the first ufologist, as it were. No surprise, then, that when Arnold Palmer, editor of *Fate* magazine, learned of a UFO report at Maury Island, Washington, involving alleged debris, he would turn to Arnold to investigate the case.

Arnold became a minor celebrity, granting numerous print and radio interviews, posing for pictures, writing articles for *Fate*, and eventually (with Palmer) his own autobiography, *The Coming of the Saucers: A Documentary Report on Sky Objects That Have Mystified the World*. All this once led ufologist and computer scientist Jacques Vallee to suggest that we might just as easily refer to the UFO phenomenon as the "Arnold phenomenon."

THE UFO REPORT

When we began this guide, we felt it would be a relatively routine matter to cull about fifty quality cases from the voluminous (and ever-growing) UFO literature. After all, we have been in the field or on its immediate periphery for upward of twenty years apiece. Individual cases came rapidly to mind, each one identified by the now familiar name of a witness or location: Arnold, Socorro, Levelland, Valensole, Trans-en-Provence, Bentwaters, Betty & Barney Hill, Pascagoula, Brooklyn Bridge, Lakenheath, Shermer, Mantell, Travis Walton, Kirtland AFB, Hudson Valley, Cash-Landrum, and so on, ad infinitum. After all, it was Hynek himself, head of the Center for UFO Studies, who had warned us of that embarrassment of riches.

But somewhat to our surprise—perhaps we were too close to the forest to distinguish individual trees—the woods weren't as littered with oaks and elms as mighty as we had initially assumed, at least not as far as reliable, detailed descriptions of the actual objects themselves were concerned. It might be more accurate to say that ufology's classic cases were, in the main, investigated and reported on during the field's formative days and in the two decades of surging enthusiasm and interest that followed, when an organization like the now moribund NICAP—the National Investigations Committee on Aerial Phenomena—could boast some 20,000 members. From its inception in 1955 until the mid-1970s, England's *Flying Saucer Review* (*FSR*), the world's oldest continually published UFO journal, was relentlessly report-oriented. Witnesses were interviewed by its far-flung correspondents, sketches solicited, photographs of locations and any existing physical traces taken, etc. In short, UFO sightings were investigated and the results published relatively shortly after the incident.

When new organizations, each with their own newsletter or journal, appeared on the scene, NICAP and *FSR* were the models to be emulated. American emulators included the now defunct Aerial Phenomena Research Organization with its *A.P.R.O. Bulletin;* MUFON, the Mutual UFO Network (*MUFON UFO Journal*);

and CUFOS, the Center for UFO Studies (*International UFO Reporter*). Even a casual perusal of back issues of these journals will reveal evidence of the *FSR* formula—the UFO report came first, followed by book reviews, commentary, letters to the editor, and related UFO ephemera. Admittedly, the quality of these reports could vary dramatically, depending on who conducted the original investigation and wrote it up for final publication.

Then a funny thing happened on the way to the Millennium. Imperceptibly, but nonetheless cumulatively, the editorial content of the UFO journals underwent a dramatic sea change. The UFO report—the published results of an actual field investigation—was gradually superceded by what might be called the UFO narrative: the sensational story in which claims and allegations are made, but few actual eyewitnesses are interviewed, and little or no additional evidence is collected or substantiated. Follow-up investigation is minimal, at best.

The classic UFO report has been crowded out by the abduction account as much as anything else, even though many of these involve no clearly observed shape or form, until the percipient reports being inside a physical object of unknown configuration, at least as far as its external form is concerned. Much historical material that should have been resolved long ago is also endlessly debated, the so-called Roswell Incident being but the most pernicious example.

Two weeks after Arnold's initial 1947 sighting, officials at Roswell Army Air Field, Roswell, New Mexico, issued a press release announcing that they had recovered, relatively intact, one of the "flying discs" that had been attracting so much attention. Later that same afternoon, in Fort Worth, Texas, a press conference was called to announce that the flying saucer was in reality a misidentified weather balloon. It was a part of Project Mogul, a highly classified project employing balloons and acoustic sensors in an attempt to monitor Soviet atomic bomb testing, though its existence was not admitted to at the time.

Buoyed by its fiftieth anniversary in 1997, the Roswell Incident has ballooned beyond all proportion. Along with allegations of alien abductions, continued government cover-up, the authenticity of the so-called MJ-12 documents, the existence of underground bases, reverse-engineered flying saucers, crop circles and animal mutilations, Roswell threatens to drive the old-fashioned UFO report into virtual extinction. Fully half of the material we see in the UFO journals these days has to do, in one way or another, with some aspect of Roswell or alleged alien abductions. Either traditional, organizational ufology has completely lost its bearings, or UFOs are no longer seen in the way they once were.

Current mainstream books and magazine articles treating the UFO phenomenon fare little better in our assessment of the contemporary situation. Indeed, they fare much worse. We were dismayed with the lack of attention and descriptive detail paid to UFO shapes. The devil *should* be in the details, but most modern commentators glance glibly over them in their rush to get to the next conspiracy theory or horror story involving extraterrestrial rape and hybrid babies, leaving the actual stimuli in the proverbial lurch. Frankly, we were troubled at how often UFOs were described (although "dismissed" would be the better word) as merely "round," "glowing," or "triangle-shaped." As any student of geometry could tell you, there is a vast visual discrepancy between right, isosceles, and equilateral triangles. Similarly, what does "kite-shaped" tell us in real terms, when terrestrial kites come shaped as everything from rectangular boxes and bats, to elongated diamonds and flying wings?

Our question, then, remains a simple but imminently fundamental one: What do these UFOs really *look* like? The question is not a trivial one, as it should provide some pretty good clues to the exact nature of the phenomenon.

CLASSIFY AND RECLASSIFY

Most attempts to classify the UFO phenomenon have been based on such general qualities that they are almost worthless when it comes to individual cases and the ability to make predictions about the phenomenon itself. Typically, they tend to fall into two broad categories. Either UFOs are classified as to shape or as to behavior. Rarely, if ever, do the two approaches intermingle in any meaningful way.

Previous attempts to classify UFO reports on the basis of shape alone left much to be desired. For example, the first official analysis of the subject in any depth divided the phenomenon into a mere four categories. In the wake of the flood of UFO reports unleashed by Arnold's landmark sighting, the U.S. Air Force initiated Project Sign to study some of these sightings. A year after its creation, Sign released a report based on the data contained in 243 domestic reports and 30 foreign ones. Project Sign grouped the objects sighted into four classifications, according to configuration:

1. Flying discs, i.e., very low aspect ratio aircraft
2. Torpedo or cigar-shaped bodies with no wings or fins visible in flight
3. Spherical or balloon-shaped objects
4. Balls of light

This Air Force effort at classification would be rather like dividing all birds, or mammals, or any other animal class, into a mere four unvarying forms, while ignoring any changes in shape that might be occasioned by circumstances of perception (lighting, angle, etc.), duration of sighting, proximity, and so on. No doubt they realized the error of their ways, however, as in 1952, the Air Force UFO project, by then renamed "Blue Book," had expanded to five items and a catchall sixth to classify all UFO shapes: (1) Elliptical, (2) Rocket & Aircraft, (3) Meteor or Comet, (4) Lenticular, Conical, or Teardrop, (5) Flame, and (6) Other Shapes. But this classification system mistakenly combined shapes and explanations in one confusing whole.

Two decades later the situation had not vastly improved. In 1966, in the second of two classic scientific studies of the phenomenon (*Challenge to Science: The UFO Enigma*), computer scientist Jacques Vallee and his co-author, wife Janine, still divided UFO sightings into four basic categories or types:

Type I: the observation of an "unusual object," spherical, discoidal, or more complex in form, on or close to the ground

Type II: the observation of an "unusual object," with vertical cylindrical formation, in the sky, associated with a diffuse cloud

Type III: the observation of an "unusual object" of spherical, discoidal, or elliptical shape stationary in the sky

Type IV: the observation of an "unusual object" moving continuously through the air, regardless of its accelerations, variations in color, or rotations

To their credit, the Vallees further refined some of these divisions. Under Type II, for example, they noted Types IIA and B. A Type IIA vertical cigar is one that moves erratically through the sky, while a Type IIB remained essentially "stationary (sic) and gives rise to secondary phenomena." Unfortunately, this kind of categorization mixes genders. Whereas Types I, II, and III all reference shape or form (and in some cases behavior), Type IV refers to behavior only. And if one categorizes Type IVs as exhibiting continuous motion, why not a Type V for all forms that exhibit *dis*continuous flight? Moreover, almost all Type II cases, the vertical cloud-cigar, are associated with the localized 1954 French flap. Maybe Vallee's own French origins are showing here. In any event, we see no reason to assign cloud cigars a stature that would rank them as one of only four "universal" UFO types.

The next significant attempt at classification came in 1972, with the publication of astronomer J. Allen Hynek's *The UFO Experience: A Scientific Inquiry*. Hynek's classification system, which involves six categories that fall into two distinct classes, gained widespread currency because of its association with the hugely successful Steven Spielberg movie, *Close Encounters of the Third Kind*.

Hynek's first class is comprised of Nocturnal Lights, Daylight Discs, and Radar-Visuals. The problem with this system is already apparent: UFOs are being largely defined in regard to the individual *circumstances* of the report, rather than in reference to the phenomenon itself. There is no compelling reason to associate a nocturnal light with a radar-visual case, for example. Nor is the Hynek system able to handle cases of daylight cigars, spheres, and egg shapes, which are reported in abundance, unless we lump these cases with Daylight Discs, in which case the label becomes a misnomer.

Hynek's second class of cases falls under the umbrella of Close Encounters. Of these, we have Close Encounters of the First, Second, and Third Kind, distinguishable from one another only by the extent of the object's interaction with the environment. Thus, a Close Encounter of the First Kind is one in which "no interaction of the UFO with the environment or the observers is reported." A Close Encounter of the Second Kind occurs when "it is reported that a UFO has left tangible evidence," and a Close Encounter of the Third Kind is one in which "animated creatures," presumably from an associated UFO, are reported.

By mixing not one or two genders, but three—appearance, circumstances, and proximity—the Hynek system results in intrinsic contradictions. For example, Hynek considers the Father Gill case (see page 52) a Close Encounter of the highest sort because animated figures were seen waving from the hovering, circular platform, which never landed. But since no photographs were taken, the evidence for the Gill sighting is wholly anecdotal. Yet a good physical trace case in which no animated entities were seen would leave more corroborating evidence, while curiously coming in second in terms of overall "ranking" or importance.

The most recent effort at a UFO classification system comes again from Vallee in his 1990 work entitled *Confrontations: A Scientist's Search for Alien Contact*. Here, Vallee publishes a much refined and revised version of his earlier classification system. The new categories consist of Anomalies (AN), Close Encounters (CE), Maneuvers (M), and Flybys (F), each with five progressing stages of severity (with 5 being the most severe). But problems persist. For example, it's conceivable under Vallee's latest system that a witness could be killed by a "bolt" of ball lightning, which would qualify as an AN (Anomalies) 5 ranking, but which would also tell us very little about the UFO phenomenon as usually perceived. Having gone from too few categories, Vallee seems to have gone to too many.

UFO GEOMETRY 101

To avoid the problems that have plagued the UFO classifications systems of the past, we have adhered to a single criteria—*form*: How was the UFO perceived and shaped, and did it convincingly change (or maintain) that form over time, that is, in ways not normally associated with a change in perception or viewing angle?

Our first type, then, is the UFO as **Lightform.** Lightforms not only encompass Hynek's nocturnal lights, but reported balls of light (BOLs), rays, columns, and cones of light, as well as light *formations* or arrays—especially when the latter is not associated with any coherent body to which the many lights seem to be affixed or attached. Thus, an otherwise visible disk or other object seen by night and described as bearing or beaming individual lights would not fall into this category. The overwhelming majority of all UFO sightings are reported as nothing more than a bright light.

Spherical UFOs are those that resemble a perfectly round sphere seen close up over time. Some are no bigger than a basketball in size; others may be larger than a house. Occasionally, these spheres may feature a base of some kind or Saturnlike rings.

Discoid is our third type. Here we include objects that remain disc-shaped in the witnesses' mind either because of the duration or proximity of the sighting. In other words, this is the "classic" flying saucer—whether domed, finned, or otherwise outfitted—seen either far from or near the reporting witness. The disc-shaped UFO has always been one of the most frequently reported UFO shapes.

Elliptical UFOs are those that are neither flattened discs nor fat cigars, but hover comfortably somewhere in the middle. They are typically described as elongated or egg-shaped, and are most frequently reported when viewed close up or already landed on the ground. These oval or "football"-shaped UFOs are often lacking in exterior features.

The **Cylindrical** type is essentially a cigar-shaped UFO. These objects are longer than they are wide. Often they display tapered or conical ends, but sometimes they have one flat end and more resemble a missile or bullet. A few cylindrical UFOs have two flat ends and look more like a fat barrel or drum than anything else. Some cigar-shaped UFOs produce a distinctive vapor trail.

Rectangular UFOs are just that—objects with squared corner angles like those of a coffin, washing machine, or refrigerator. They are largely, but not exclusively, a Brazilian and South American phenomenon. They can be as small as a "flying carpet" or as large as an aircraft carrier. They are seen infrequently.

Triangular UFOs seem to be on the upsweep. Relatively rare if not nonexistent in the early days of ufology, they now account for an inordinate number of all UFO reports. Included in this type are top-shaped, diamond-shaped, and cone-shaped objects, as well as flying wings or "boomerangs." While triangular UFOs are frequently reported as large and low-flying, they are rarely if ever reported as actually resting upon the ground.

Shape-shifters are those UFOs that convincingly alter form over time in ways that can't be easily attributed to perceptual angle or a simple case of "mistaken identity." Their importance lies in the fact that many shape-shifters cast doubt on the literal, physical nature of the phenomenon, leaving the window open for alternative theories of origin.

While a few reported UFO shapes may not fit into our eight types, we are confident that our classification system is broad enough to encompass more than 99 percent of all UFO sightings reported. As far as a classification system goes, this is as good as it gets.

ON WITH THE SHOW

To accommodate the phenomenon's vast time scale and many varying physical appearances and manifestations, we have sought out UFO cases from a wide variety of sources. In preparing our case descriptions for this field guide, we have come to appreciate just how difficult it is to translate a transient event, glimpsed under circumstances that are rarely ideal, into a coherent "portrait." Accordingly, our sympathies for and appreciation of those investigators and researchers who preceded us. Wherever possible, we've relied on previously published accounts by those same investigators and sources we consider reliable, and which were accompanied by original witness sketches or sketches based on the witness's description. Our artist has used both sources to create his own visual interpretation of the reported phenomenon.

LIGHTFORM
UFOs

TYPE: *Lightform*	**DESCRIPTIVE INCIDENT**
VARIANT: *Green fireball*	**DATE:** *December 5, 1948*
SKEPTIC'S SOLUTION: *Flares and*	**LOCATION:** *Albuquerque, New Mexico*
meteors	**WITNESSES:** *Captain Goede, his co-*
	pilot, and engineer; another pilot

In late November, people around Albuquerque began reporting seeing "green streaks" in the sky at night. The Air Force wrote off the sightings as being due to flares brought home and shot off by thousands of GIs back from the war. But the events of December fifth forced the Air Force to reconsider their flare theory.

At 9:27 that night the crew of a USAF C-47 was startled by a green ball of fire that flashed across the sky as the transport plane was flying at 18,000 feet about ten miles east of Albuquerque. It *looked* like a meteor except that it was huge, very green, and flew without arching downward, as meteors normally do. In fact, the fireball had started out low near the Sandia Mountains, arched upward a little, then leveled out, according to Captain Goede, his co-pilot, and engineer. Since the crew had seen an identical object twenty-two minutes before near Las Vegas, they called Kirtland Air Force Base to report the incident.

Just minutes later Kirtland received a call from the captain of a Pioneer Airlines DC-3 saying that he and his co-pilot had seen a green ball of fire east of Las Vegas at 9:35. They first thought it was a meteor, but then realized that its trajectory was too flat for a meteor. The fireball had approached the plane head-on, changing color from orange-red to green. Since the object appeared to be on collision course, the captain pulled the DC-3 up into a tight turn. At its largest, the fireball was bigger than a full moon, but then began falling toward the ground, getting dimmer until it disappeared. Kirtland received calls on the green fireball from all over northern New Mexico that night.

Since this "Land of Enchantment" was the site of most atomic weapons development in the United States, Air Force intelligence expressed considerable concern over these events. They immediately called in Lincoln La Paz, director of New Mexico's Institute of Meteoritics, to investigate. He determined that a total of eight green fireballs had been seen, and plotted the impact point of the most spectacular of these sightings, the December fifth event. But a search of the suspected impact area repeatedly failed to turn up any physical evidence, and La Paz began to seriously doubt that the green fireballs were meteorites.

Within days the green fireballs resumed their almost nightly appearances, and continued doing so through January, 1949. This gave just about everyone, including La Paz, intelligence officers from Kirtland Air Force Base, and some of the most distinguished scientists at Los Alamos, a chance to see the objects. By mid-February the Air Force knew the objects were real but still had no idea what they were. So they called a conference, which was attended by such people as Edward Teller, father of the H-bomb. La Paz argued strongly against the meteor explanation, and two days later the Air Force concluded that the green fireballs were an unknown natural phenomenon of some kind.

By the summer of 1949, La Paz was put in charge of Project Twinkle, which was designed to photograph the phenomenon with three cine-theodolite stations. But after a year and a half Twinkle was deemed a failure, due to a lack of funds and cameras because of the start of the Korean War. By the end of 1952 the green fireballs had stopped appearing over New Mexico.

SOURCE: *Edward J. Ruppelt,* The Report on Unidentified Flying Objects, *(New York: Ace, 1956).*

TYPE: *Lightform*	**DESCRIPTIVE INCIDENT**
VARIANT: *Lights in V-formation*	**DATE:** *August 25, 1951*
SKEPTIC'S SOLUTION: *Migrating birds*	**LOCATION:** *Lubbock, Texas*
illuminated by streetlights	**WITNESSES:** *Professors W. I. Robinson,*
	A. G. Oberg, W. L. Ducker, Dr.
	George, others

On a steamy summer night in Texas, four college professors were sitting outdoors, sipping tea and discussing micrometeorites. The group included professors of geology, physics, and chemical engineering, and the head of the petroleum engineering department at nearby Texas Technological College. "If a group had been handpicked to observe a UFO," noted Edward Ruppelt, then director of Project Blue Book, "we couldn't have picked a more technically qualified group of people."

What the four saw would stand Air Force investigators on their collective head. At 9:20 P.M. a formation of softly glowing, bluish-green lights sailed swiftly overhead. Surprised by the sight, the four pooled notes. All agreed on the color of the lights, that they were grouped in a semicircle, and traveled from north to south. But the number of estimated lights ranged from fifteen to thirty.

To their even greater surprise, less than an hour later the experience repeated itself! Duration and direction were similar, but this time no organized pattern was discernible; the lights were simply grouped in irregular clumps.

The professors wondered if lightning could strike the same spot twice, why not a third time, and so agreed to meet the following evening. The lights obliged, resulting in a nightly vigil that would be repeated for the next two weeks. Two more colleagues were invited to the "skywatch," and the group was rewarded with ten additional sightings. The lights routinely flashed into view halfway above the northern horizon, traversed ninety degrees of sky in three seconds, and disappeared halfway above the southern horizon.

By now hundreds of people had reported seeing the "Lubbock Lights." One of these, Carl Hart, Jr., a Texas Tech freshman and amateur photographer, even produced a photograph of the lights. Hart told Ruppelt that on the night of August 31 he had pushed his bed next to an open window in order to better view the night sky. He'd been lying down less than half an hour when the lights flew over. Hart then took his loaded 35mm camera into the backyard, hoping for a reappearance. The lights did reappear, and young Hart managed to snap two pictures.

A few minutes later the lights flew overhead a third time and Hart took three more pictures.

The best of these pictures, widely reprinted in the UFO literature and elsewhere, revealed two lines of globular lights, fifteen in all, comprising a distinct flattened V-formation—something the professors claimed they had never seen after their first sighting. Although a large "flying wing" with numerous pairs of lights had been reported over Albuquerque, New Mexico, twenty minutes prior to the first Lubbock sighting, Air Force analysis of Hart's original negatives suggested that the lights were not attached to a single underlying object.

SOURCE: *Edward J. Ruppelt,* The Report on Unidentified Flying Objects *(New York: Ace, 1956).*

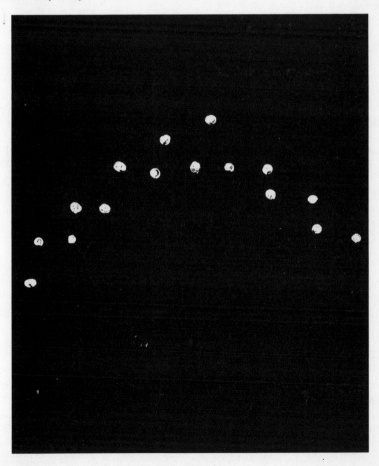

SPHERICAL UFOs

TYPE: *Spherical*
VARIANT: *Featureless sphere*
SKEPTIC'S SOLUTION: *None*

DESCRIPTIVE INCIDENT
DATE: *Summer 1945*
LOCATION: *Northeast Pacific Ocean*
WITNESSES: *Robert S. Crawford and other crewmen*

The U.S. Army transport ship *Delarof,* having dropped off munitions and supplies in Alaska, was now on the open sea, heading back to Seattle. One day at sunset, Robert S. Crawford, who served as an Army radioman aboard the ship, was standing on the port side near the radio room when he heard shouts from the crew. As he turned around he saw a large round object rising above the water. Other crewmen had actually witnessed the object emerge from the sea about a mile or so from the *Delarof.*

The sphere, which showed darkly against the setting sun, climbed straight up for a few moments then broke into level flight and began to circle the ship. Many crewmen observed the enormous object, which they estimated measured about 150 to 200 feet in diameter. Though the object was clearly within range of the ship's guns, the gun crews held their fire, still alert for any signs of hostility.

The object circled the ship two or three times, according to Crawford, who reported the encounter many years later while studying to be a geologist at the University of North Dakota. Making no audible sound, the object moved smoothly and was unaffected by the strong winds. Several minutes later it disappeared to the south or southwest. The crew then saw three flashes of light coming from the area where the object had vanished. Puzzled and concerned over the incident, the captain of the *Delarof* posted an extra watch when the ship passed through that sector later, but the strange object was not seen again.

SOURCE: *Anonymous, "The Question of Submerging UFOs," The UFO Investigator, 4(5): 4, March 1968.*

29

TYPE: *Spherical*
VARIANT: *Sphere with "skirt"*
SKEPTIC'S SOLUTION: *Hoax*

DESCRIPTIVE INCIDENT
DATE: *17:45 GMT, January 27, 1978*
LOCATION: *Frodsham, Cheshire, England*
WITNESSES: *Anonymous*

While poaching for pheasant one night on the banks of the River Weaver, four youths from Frodsham, ages seventeen to nineteen, were stationed in an area known locally as the Devil's Garden, a wide expanse of fields and lush vegetation bordering the Mersey Estuary. One of the foursome was startled to see a silver sphere—which he first assumed to be an out-of-control satellite—approaching from the southeast and skimming no more than twenty feet above the surface of the water. It was giving off an odd combination of sounds, a faint humming mixed with the sigh of rushing wind.

All four watched as the object passed their position and then settled into some bushes nearby. Approaching, they spied a round, sphere-shaped object, approximately fifteen feet across. Flashing lights were seen on the visible side of the sphere, along with a series of windows from which shone a brilliant "fuzzy" light, rendering the interior impervious to inspection. The bottom of the sphere was encircled by a short flange or skirt, from which flames (retro-rockets?) had briefly flared as the object landed. Shortly all outward illumination ceased, plunging the landscape into darkness.

Fearing contamination, as a Soviet satellite with radioactive components had recently crashed in Canada, the four were preparing to flee when a figure in a silver, one-piece suit walked out from behind the "satellite." Atop the figure's head or helmet was something resembling a miner's lamp which gave off a bright violet light. The figure appeared to acknowledge a herd of grazing cows in a nearby field, then retreated behind the sphere, only to reemerge immediately with another silver-suited figure. Both were now bearing a large cage of some sort, seemingly composed of thin, aluminumlike bars in a vertical and horizontal pattern.

They approached one of the standing cows, which remained stationary, and placed the cage over it. Then they proceeded to slide the cage's struts and bars about the cow's body, as if conducting a series of calculated measurements. At this stage, wondering whether they might be measured next, the four decided to flee the scene. No one saw the object depart.

As they ran away, one of the four reported a tugging in his testicles. The next day his testicles were still sore and the surrounding area red and tender. That embarrassing detail, coupled with the fact that the four were trespassing in the first place, prevented them from going public with their identities. Eventually, however, the story made its way into a small, local weekly newspaper and from there into the hands of English ufologists.

SOURCE: *Jenny Randles and Paul Whetnall, "Four Young Men and a UFO," Flying Saucer Review, Vol. 26, No. 3, pp. 5–7, September, 1980.*

TYPE: *Spherical*	**DESCRIPTIVE INCIDENT**
VARIANT: *Sphere with "Saturn ring"*	**DATE:** *October 25, 1973*
SKEPTIC'S SOLUTION: *None*	**LOCATION:** *North West Cape, Western Australia*
	WITNESSES: *Unnamed*

On October 6, 1973, the "Yom Kippur" war broke out in the Middle East. Cold War tensions escalated, and on the evening of October 25, U.S. forces worldwide were put on full nuclear alert. U.S. nuclear submarines in the Indian and Pacific Oceans received the alert from the U.S. Naval Communication Station, located on Western Australia's remote North West Cape and operated by America's super-secret National Security Agency.

Also that evening, at about 7:30, two independent U.S. Navy personnel spotted a mysterious intruder in the airspace over that highly restricted base. A lieutenant commander driving to the nearby town of Exmouth saw "a large black, airborne object" hovering at an altitude of about 2,000 feet. It was about five miles to the west and made no noise. Less than thirty seconds later the object shot away to the north at "unbelievable speed," leaving no exhaust.

Meanwhile, a fire captain was driving toward the officers' club when he noticed a large dark object in the sky. After first thinking it must be a small cloud formation, he decided to stop his pickup truck and got out for a better look. For several minutes he watched the object hover in the pale, green-blue sky, which he realized was totally free of any clouds. The black sphere measured about thirty feet in diameter and stood absolutely stationary less than a thousand feet above the ground. Its only feature was a one-foot-thick halo that revolved or pulsated through the middle—or because of perspective, just below the middle—of the object. His sketch of the object shows it had a typical, Saturnlike shape.

Then, without warning, the object took off toward the north at tremendous speed. Though the Americans reportedly investigated the sightings, no explanation was ever found—or, at least, offered to their Australian hosts.

SOURCE: *Bill Chalker,* The OZ Files *(Potts Point, Australia: Duffy & Snellgrove, 1996).*

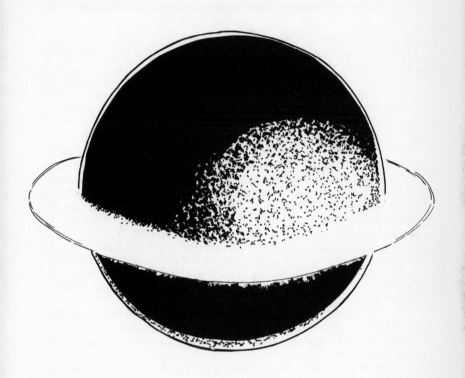

TYPE: *Spherical*	**DESCRIPTIVE INCIDENT**
VARIANT: *Sphere with square ring*	**DATE:** *July 7, 1989*
SKEPTIC'S SOLUTION: *None*	**LOCATION:** *Kanazawa, Japan*
	WITNESSES: *Yasuhiko Hamazaki, Mrs.*
	Hamazaki, and daughter

Yasuhiko Hamazaki was standing outside his house about a half hour before sunset when his young daughter pointed at something in the sky and said: "What's that?" Because it seemed to have an unusual shape and moved at such a low altitude, Hamazaki thought it might be a hot air balloon. But hearing none of the whooshing sound that such a balloon's "blowtorch" normally makes, Hamazaki decided it must be something unusual and ran inside to get his video camera.

Hamazaki told his wife about the object as he grabbed an old videotape and ran out to his garden, where he hoped to get a better view of it. As his wife looked on through binoculars, Hamazaki started up the 8mm video camera. Initially, he had some difficulty getting the object in his field of view, then zoomed in and out before finally managing to get a distinct object in the viewfinder. At 34 seconds into the tape the object has a squarish outline and looks somewhat like a sphere with an extremely bright, square-cut card through the middle.

Meanwhile, Mrs. Hamazaki had observed the object fall and rise in altitude and commented on its flashing red and blue lights. Her husband continued taping the object as it traveled a straight path to the horizon, finally becoming too faint and small to see through the viewfinder. In all, he taped the object for 55 seconds.

The Hamazaki sighting was investigated by local news reporters. The air base nearby never had radar contact with the object, and the regional meteorologist said there had been no weather balloons in the area at the time.

Though reports of Saturn-shaped objects with a square ring like Hamazaki's are rare in the UFO literature, more than a decade earlier a nearly identical object was photographed by two teachers from Minneapolis, Michael Lindstrom and his wife, as they were vacationing on Maui in Hawaii on January 2, 1975. The three pictures snapped by Lindstrom show a white or silver sphere with a dark square ring around it. "The similarities between the UFO images in these two cases are obvious and surprising," noted physicist and UFO investigator Bruce Maccabee, "when one considers the dearth of other cases in which different persons have photographed nearly identical UFOs at widely different times and places."

SOURCE: *Bruce Maccabee, "A Rare Photo Coincidence,"* International UFO Reporter, *May/June 1990.*

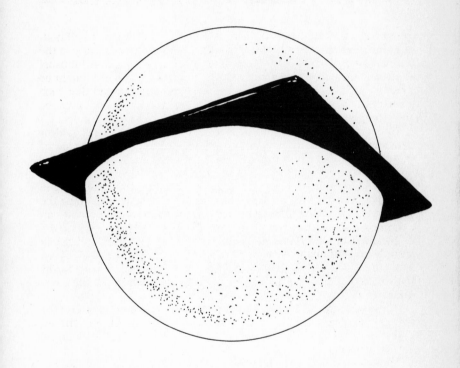

DISCOID
UFOs

TYPE: *Discoid*	**DESCRIPTIVE INCIDENT**
VARIANT: *Double ring*	**DATE:** *March 31, 1952*
SKEPTIC'S SOLUTION: *Smoke rings*	**LOCATION:** *Greenfield, Massachusetts*
	WITNESS: *Charles T. Early*

Charles Early was burning leaves in his backyard on a clear and windless Sunday afternoon when he heard the kind of swishing sound a storm makes as it approaches. Early looked up to see if the wind might spread the bonfire onto his two nearby barns and saw two large rings in the sky, parallel to one another and about four feet apart. The rings were as bright as polished chrome. Each one was about four inches thick and thirty feet in diameter.

The rings came zooming down toward Early so rapidly that he was certain they would hit the ground. But they did not. Just before reaching the ground, the rings, which never changed their relative position to one another and spun in a clockwise direction, rose back up into the sky and came to a hover over Early. The rings, which seemed to emit a humming sound, then turned from a horizontal to vertical position, moved south about fifty feet, and returned to a horizontal position. After hovering for about a minute, the rings began to pick up speed. Initially, the rings moved irregularly and only achieved smooth flight after attaining jet speed.

The pair of rings, which were headed for a factory chimney, shot up toward a large mountain about six miles away. They then banked, turned and headed back toward Early. But a quarter of a mile away, the rings suddenly shot upward at a speed estimated at 1,500 miles per hour, and disappeared from sight within a second.

Other double-ringed and single-ringed objects—sometimes partially hidden in a cloud or seen with a spindle through the center—have been reported in the UFO literature. A black ring is all that remained of an apparently solid disc-shaped object in the fourth frame of a set of four UFO photographs taken by Rex Heflin on August 3, 1965, in California. But perhaps the best known case of this kind involved a black ring seen and photographed over Fort Belvoir, Virginia, by a private in the Army in September, 1957. In his sequence of photographs, a fluffy cloud gradually forms around, and eventually hides, the flying black ring. This case was eventually explained as the by-product of an "atom bomb simulation demonstration" on the base.

SOURCE: *Ralph Rankow, "The Ring-Shaped UFO,"* Flying Saucers: UFO Report, No. 4, 1967.

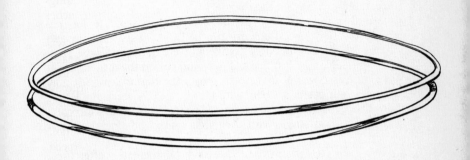

TYPE: *Discoid*	**DESCRIPTIVE INCIDENT**
VARIANT: *Discs in formation*	**DATE:** *July 14, 1952*
SKEPTIC'S SOLUTION: *None*	**LOCATION:** *Norfolk, Virginia*
	WITNESSES: *Capt. William B. Nash, Third Officer William Fortenberry*

On a clear night with unlimited visibility, a Pan American DC-4 was at an altitude of 8,000 feet over Chesapeake Bay, en route to Miami from New York. At the controls were pilot William Nash and co-pilot William Fortenberry. At about 8:00 P.M. both saw a reddish glow in the distance, rapidly closing on their plane.

As it drew nearer, the glow resolved itself into six separate fiery red objects. Just as they passed underneath the DC-4, all six suddenly and simultaneously flipped on edge. "While all were in the edgewise position," Nash noted, "the last five slid over and passed the leader so that the echelon was now tail first, so to speak, the top or last craft now being nearest our position. Then, without any arc or swerve at all, they all flipped back together to the flat attitude and darted off in a direction that formed a sharp angle with their first course, holding their new formation."

To their even greater surprise, Nash said, "Immediately after these six lined away, two more objects just like them darted out from behind and under our airplane at the same altitude as the others." All eight objects blinked off, back on, and then off again as they finally disappeared in the distance.

Captain Nash reported the objects as definitely disc-shaped. Their "edges were well-defined," he said, "not phosphorescent or fuzzy in the least . . . In shape and proportion, they were much like coins." As they flipped on edge, according to Nash, "The sides to the left of us [went] up and the glowing surfaces [faced] right. Though the bottom surfaces did not become clearly visible, we had the impression that they were unlighted. The exposed edges, also unlighted, appeared to be about fifteen thick, and the top surface, at least, seemed flat." Their diameter was estimated at 100 feet.

SOURCE: *Ronald D. Story*, UFOs and the Limits of Science *(New York: William Morrow and Company, 1981).*

TYPE: *Discoid*	**DESCRIPTIVE INCIDENT**
VARIANT: *"Coin"*	**DATE:** *March 20, 1950*
SKEPTIC'S SOLUTION: *None*	**LOCATION:** *Little Rock, Arkansas*
	WITNESSES: *Jack Adams, G. W. Anderson Jr.*

When it comes to experienced observers of the sky, airline pilots are among the best. For this reason there is little reason to doubt what Captain Jack Adams and his co-pilot, Reserve Air Force pilot G. W. Anderson Jr., saw that night shortly before 9:30 on their Chicago and Southern Airlines flight. The plane was flying at 2,000 feet on a southwesterly course about fifteen miles north of Little Rock, when Adams directed Anderson's attention to an object that was rapidly approaching them from the south on a north heading.

The object was circular with a diameter of about 100 feet. On top was a blindingly bright, blue-white light that blinked about three times per second. As the object passed in front of the airliner in a straight line, the pilots estimated its speed to be in excess of a thousand miles per hour. At its closest approach—a thousand feet higher and about a half mile distant from the plane—the pilots saw the bottom of the craft, which had nine to twelve oval ports or openings located near its outer circumference. A soft purple light shone through these "ports."

The entire sighting lasted no more than about thirty seconds. Though the pilots believed they had seen a secret experimental craft, Air Force investigators could not explain the sighting. It is listed as one of the 701 "Unknowns" in the Project Blue Book files.

SOURCE: *Brad Steiger (ed.),* Project Blue Book *(New York: Ballantine, 1976); Richard Hall,* The UFO Evidence *(Washington, D.C.: NICAP, 1964).*

TYPE: *Discoid*	DESCRIPTIVE INCIDENT
VARIANT: *Disc with central cylinder*	DATE: *June 1952*
SKEPTIC'S SOLUTION: *None*	LOCATION: *Hasselbacht, [East] Germany*
	WITNESSES: *Oscar and Gabrielle Linke and others unnamed*

As an adventure, Oscar Linke's narrow escape into West Berlin with his wife and six children positively paled in comparison to what had happened to him shortly before he left Soviet-occupied East Germany. According to a sworn affidavit he signed before a West Berlin judge on July 1, 1952, Linke, who was then forty-eight, was returning home with his eleven-year-old stepdaughter when a tire blew out on his motorcycle near the town of Hasselbacht.

As they walked into town at twilight, Gabrielle pointed to something happening 150 feet away in the woods. When Oscar went to investigate, he came across two men dressed in shiny metallic clothing less than fifty feet away from him. The men were stooped over and looking at something on the ground. As Oscar approached to within a dozen feet, he looked over a fence and saw a large object "resembling a huge frying pan" on the ground in the clearing below. The object was about fifty feet in diameter and had two rows of holes, each about a foot across, along the periphery. Atop the metallic object was a black cylindrical tower a little more than three feet high.

When Gabrielle, who was a short distance behind Oscar, called out, the two "men" immediately jumped into the tower and disappeared inside. One of the men, noted Oscar, had a lamp on the front of his body which lit up at regular intervals. Suddenly, the object began to glitter, change color from green to red, and issue a slight hum. As the light and noise increased, the tower slid down into the center of the object, which rose slowly and spun like a top. The object, now surrounded by a ring of flames, seemed to be resting on the cylindrical tower that had just passed through the center of the object.

The object then lifted slowly off the ground, and the cylinder on which it had just rested appeared atop the object again. As the disc continued to climb, it made a whistling sound, only to disappear finally over Stockholm. A shepherd a mile from the woods also saw the object fly away, as did a watchman at a nearby sawmill. But to assure himself that he had not been dreaming, Oscar then went to where the object had been and found a freshly dug hole in the ground—in the exact shape of the "conning tower" he had just seen on the object.

In telling the judge this story, Oscar assured him: "I had never heard of the term flying saucers before I escaped the Soviet zone into western Berlin." Flying saucer stories from around the world filled the pages of western newspapers during that summer of 1952.

SOURCE: *J. Allen Hynek*, The Hynek UFO Report *(New York: Dell, 1977).*

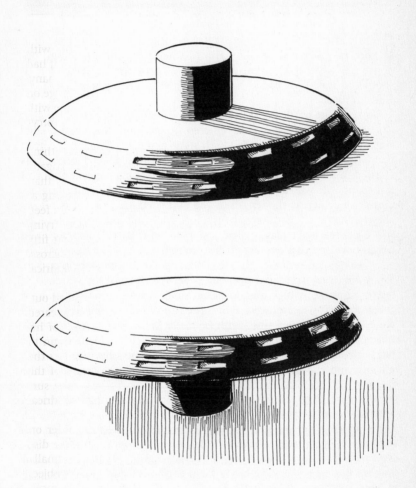

TYPE: *Discoid*	DESCRIPTIVE INCIDENT
VARIANT: *"Pancake" with windows*	DATE: *January 12, 1975*
SKEPTIC'S SOLUTION: *None*	LOCATION: *North Bergen, New Jersey*
	WITNESSES: *George O'Barski, Bill Pawlowski, others*

Shortly after 1:00 A.M., George O'Barski locked the doors of the liquor store he co-owned in Manhattan's Chelsea district. A tough, no-nonsense, seventy-two-year-old New Yorker—and a teetotaler, it should be noted—O'Barski then proceeded to drive home across the Hudson River.

To avoid the traffic lights in New Jersey, he routinely passed through North Hudson Park. But as he entered the park on this unseasonably warm night, his car radio filled with static and died. Through the open window he then heard a droning sound. When he looked left he was startled to see an object that "looked like a great big pancake that had puffed up." It was about thirty feet long, six feet high, and brightly illuminated. Across the length of the object was a series of windows about a foot apart, each one about a foot wide and four feet tall. When the object reached a playing field just ahead of O'Barski, it stopped and began hovering, just ten feet off the ground.

What happened next frightened O'Barski like never before in his life. From a narrow panel that opened up between two of the windows, a ladder came out, which nine to eleven small figures then used to reach the ground. The figures were about three and a half to four feet tall and wore one-piece "snowsuits" with hoods or helmets that covered their heads. The little men then used their "little shovels" to fill up the "little bags," which they carried, with dirt. Moments later they climbed back aboard, and the droning object rose quickly and disappeared to the north.

The experience, which lasted about four minutes, had so shaken O'Barski that he went straight to bed instead of stopping for a bite to eat at an all-night restaurant as was his habit. The next day, hoping to convince himself that he had been dreaming, he returned to the park. And there he found about fifteen little holes in the ground, each about four to five inches wide and six inches deep. Visibly upset, O'Barski finally told his son the story.

Months later O'Barski reluctantly began telling one of his liquor store customers the story. The customer—and store neighbor—was Budd Hopkins, who would later become a well-known researcher of the

UFO abduction phenomenon. When Hopkins and others began investigating O'Barski's story, they located several other witnesses who had seen the object that night from the Stonehenge Apartments, just three hundred yards or so from the site of the incident. One witness, resident Bill Pawlowski, had seen some unusual lights at about two in the morning. He described the ten to fifteen evenly spaced lights as being set horizontally in a shape he could not make out. Moments later he heard a high-pitched vibration, followed immediately by a crack. When he looked around, he noticed a break in the lobby window near his feet. He phoned the police and two officers came to investigate, but fearing ridicule, Pawlowski said nothing about the mysterious lights he had just seen.

SOURCE: *Budd Hopkins, "Sane Citizen Sees UFO in New Jersey,"* The Village Voice *21(9): 12–13, March 1, 1976.*

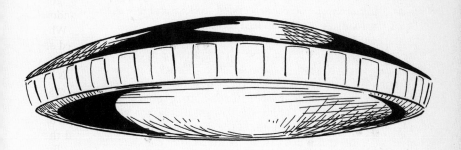

TYPE: *Discoid*
VARIANT: *Disc with "fins"*
SKEPTIC'S SOLUTION: *None*

DESCRIPTIVE INCIDENT
DATE: *September 19, 1961*
LOCATION: *Groveton, New Hampshire*
WITNESSES: *Betty and Barney Hill*

To the couple in the car traveling south on Highway 3, just below the Canadian border that night at 11:00 P.M., it appeared first as a single, distant point of light, perhaps a star or satellite. But then it did a most unstarlike thing, not only pacing the car, but perceptibly drawing closer. Still at a great distance, but now viewed through binoculars, a series of flashing red, amber, green, and blue lights could be discerned, all attached to a cigar-shaped object.

Over the next few minutes the object drew even nearer. As Betty Hill peered through their binoculars while her husband continued driving, the various colored lights ceased blinking, only to be replaced by a whitish glow coming from a double row of windows. From each end of the object a fin or appendage began slowly emerging, tipped with a red light. Ultimately, the object descended so close and low as to effectively block the roadway a few hundred feet ahead.

Barney Hill stopped the car, took the binoculars from his wife, and stepped outside for a better view. The object was now visible as a huge, glowing circular disc, somewhat like a thick, luminous pancake. Through the double row of window panes—occupying the thickness of the perimeter now directly facing him—Barney could see several figures apparently staring back at him. The thought that he was about to be "captured" raced through his mind. At the same time, the flares or fins with their red lights continued extending from either end of the object. Next, a ladder or ramp of some sort descended from beneath the object.

At this point a panicked Barney rushed back to the car, slipped it into gear, and sped away. An odd, beeping noise was heard, but the object itself could no longer be seen. Disturbed by the sighting itself, and unable to account for a considerable period of "missing time," the Hills eventually contacted Boston psychotherapist Dr. Benjamin Simon.

Under hypnosis, the Hills would "remember" being taken aboard a large, disc-shaped object where they were both subjected to rude physical examination by apparently extraterrestrial beings. Despite numerous internal differences between their two experiences, the event would be taken as the fundamental template for all future UFO abductions.

SOURCE: *John G. Fuller,* The Interrupted Journey *(New York, The Dial Press, 1966).*

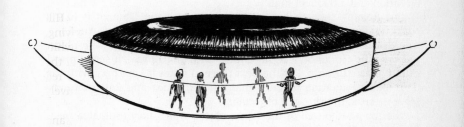

TYPE: *Discoid*
VARIANT: *Disc with rotating cupola*
SKEPTIC'S SOLUTION: *None*

DESCRIPTIVE INCIDENT
DATE: *June 1984*
LOCATION: *Mediterranean Sea*
WITNESSES: *Alexander Globa, Sergey Bolotov, Captain Solovsky*

On a calm day at sea, the Russian tanker *Gori* was twenty nautical miles east of Gibraltar and heading west. Seaman Alexander Globa and Mate Sergey Bolotov began their watch on the bridge at 4:00 P.M. While Globa was fetching binoculars, Bolotov spotted what he thought was an airplane approaching the ship's stern at about thirty degrees elevation and 5,000 feet high.

But Bolotov soon realized it wasn't an airplane. Though it had a shiny, gray metal surface, it was shaped like a "frying pan turned upside down" and emitted bright, irregular flashes of light. The object followed the tanker on a zigzag course until at 4:12 P.M., it sped up and caught up to the ship. For the next three minutes it kept pace with the *Gori*, making gyrating motions that allowed Globa and Bolotov to observe its structure through binoculars.

The top and bottom of the round object, which they estimated measured about 75 feet in diameter, appeared to be rotating slowly in opposite directions. The rosy, neonlike glow they had seen from a distance appeared to come from a cylindrical object like a tailpipe at the junction of the two rotating segments. The top portion of the object had a red cupola or dome as well as a rotating black trident-shaped feature below it. The yellow lower half of the object had lights that looked like portholes on its circumference. On the very bottom was a large round black spot surrounded by three smaller pie-shaped spots in a triangular arrangement.

A few minutes later the object stopped its gyrations and began moving toward the southwest, all the while emitting a red to yellow light. But suddenly the UFO flew over to an approaching ship and began hovering over it. The entire crew of the *Gori* was watching the object by this time, including Captain Solovsky, who contacted the approaching vessel. This Egyptian dry cargo ship, which was heading for Greece, confirmed the object's presence.

A minute or so later the object began moving back toward the *Gori*, climbing at a forty-five-degree angle. It then veered to the right, and shining "like a steel blade," shot off through the clouds until it was lost to view. The entire encounter had lasted twelve minutes.

SOURCE: **Sergey Romanov, "Disc with Rotating Cupola Observed Near Straits of Gibraltar by Russian Ship in 1984,"** International UFO Reporter, *May–June 1993.*

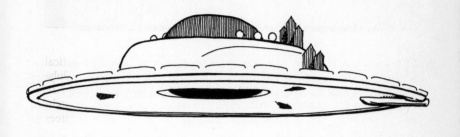

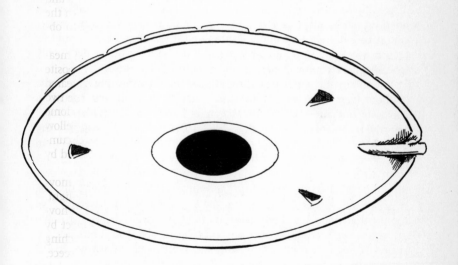

TYPE: *Discoid*	**DESCRIPTIVE INCIDENT**
VARIANT: *Disc with platform and*	**DATE:** *June 26, 1959*
"handrail"	**LOCATION:** *Papua–New Guinea*
SKEPTIC'S SOLUTION: *Venus*	**WITNESS:** *Father William Gill and*
	dozens of others

On a Friday evening, Father William Booth Gill, an Anglican missionary in the village of Boianai, Papua–New Guinea, stepped outside his mission house to view the planet Venus, which had been quite prominent the last several days. What he saw next was a bright, sparkling light above Venus that slowly drew closer.

Gill called out two colleagues who hailed others in turn. Eventually, a crowd of thirty-eight men were staring up at the strange spectacle overhead. The light had now resolved into a very large circular disc with four outwardly angled appendages, or "legs," at each "corner" of the disc. Gill would later guess its angular size as that of five full moons lined up side by side. Atop the disc, on a slightly raised platform encircled by a handrail, four oddly illuminated humanlike figures could be seen at work. By turn, one or more would disappear below deck, only to subsequently return and go about their topside business.

Eventually the object rose through low clouds, vanishing from view. An hour later, however, several smaller UFOs returned, leading Gill to conclude that the much larger disc may have been a "mother ship." Shortly, it returned, too. Finally, about 10:50 P.M., all the objects were obscured by clouds. Overall, the initial sighting had lasted more than four hours, an unusual length of time for any UFO event.

In an equally curious deviation from the "norm," the following evening the perceived "mother ship," accompanied by two smaller objects, revisited the mission home. Again, the figures busied themselves, save for one that stood with both hands on the rail, seemingly peering down at Father Gill's group, which now numbered about a dozen. Impulsively, Gill said, "I stretched my arm above my head and waved. To our surprise the figure did the same." Gill and another member of his party continued waving, all four aboard the UFO responding in turn. "There *seemed* to be no doubt that our movements were answered," Gill declared.

As the sky turned dark, a flashlight was fetched, then directed at the mother ship and switched on and off. The UFO again seemed to respond, by moving from side to side like a pendulum. Gill and group continued waving and blinking the flashlight. "Then the UFO began slowly to become bigger," Gill recalled, "apparently coming in our direction. It ceased after perhaps half a minute and came no further. After a further delay [of] two or three minutes the figures apparently lost interest in us, for they disappeared below deck."

Gill's group lost interest as well and went inside to eat dinner. The UFO could still be seen thirty minutes later, although at a greater distance. Forty-five minutes later, after church service, it had disappeared altogether. As many as eight UFOs were glimpsed the following evening, but no occupants were seen on the last occasion.

SOURCE: *Jerome Clark,* The UFO Book *(Detroit: Visible Ink Press, 1998).*

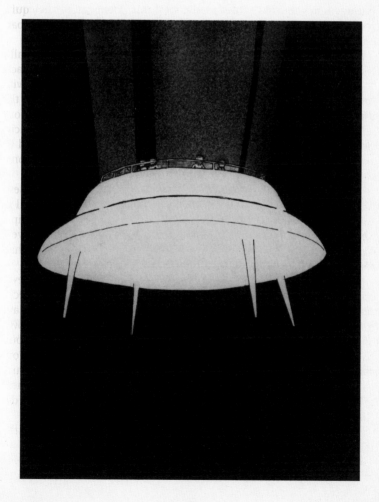

TYPE: *Discoid*
VARIANT: *Disc with asymmetrical feature*
SKEPTIC'S SOLUTION: *Hoax*

DESCRIPTIVE INCIDENT
DATE: *May 11, 1950*
LOCATION: *McMinnville, Oregon*
WITNESSES: *Mr. and Mrs. Paul Trent*

Mrs. Trent was feeding rabbits in her backyard at about 7:30 P.M. when she noticed a strange object in the northeast. She called out to her husband Paul, fetching him from the kitchen. While the object continued moving slowly toward the west, Mr. Trent ran to their car, where he thought he had left his camera. Mrs. Trent found it in the house instead.

Snatching the camera from his wife, Paul snapped off a quick shot. Thirty seconds later he took a second one. He then ran inside to get his mother-in-law. Receiving no immediate reply, he rushed back outside, barely in time to watch the object vanish in the direction of the setting sun.

Trent would later describe the superstructure of the object as "like a good-sized parachute canopy without the strings, only silvery-bright mixed with bronze." Situated roughly in the center of the pictured canopy atop the circular disc was an upright triangular appendage or "antenna." He estimated the object's diameter as between twenty and thirty feet. He heard no sound, nor did he see any exhaust, flame, or smoke emitted in the course of the sighting.

After finishing the roll on Mother's Day, the witnesses had the film developed, but were reluctant to seek publicity for the resulting UFO photos. Paul Trent in particular, thinking he might have photographed something secret, preferred to avoid any further involvement. Only after a newspaper reporter learned of the photos from two town bankers—both of whom were willing to vouch for the Trents' veracity—did word of the sighting become public. Eventually their pictures appeared in *Life* magazine, subsequently becoming staples in the UFO literature.

Some seventeen years later the Trents, typified as "very industrious farm people," would be reinterviewed by investigators from the University of Colorado, then under contract from the Air Force to investigate and analyze UFO sightings. No evidence would emerge that the original negatives had been tampered with. In conclusion, they added, "all factors investigated, geometric, psychological, and physical, appear to be consistent with the assertion that an extraordinary flying object, silvery, metallic, disc-shaped, tens of meters in diameter, and evidently artificial flew within sight of two witnesses."

Though certain discrepancies in the Trents' story—along with a visible telephone wire from which a model UFO could have been easily suspended—led some skeptics to suspect a calculated hoax, the Colorado investigators ultimately argued against a fabrication. A similar object was photographed by a pilot over Rouen, France, in the summer of 1954. In both instances, the object displayed a rim, a sloping structure above this rim, and a projection from the top that is, curiously, not centered.

SOURCE: *Daniel S. Gillmor, editor,* Scientific Study of Unidentified Flying Objects *(New York: Bantam, 1969).*

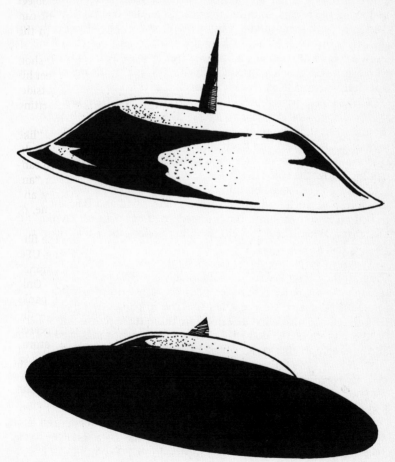

TYPE: *Discoid*
VARIANT: *"Scoutship" with undercarriage feature*
SKEPTIC'S SOLUTION: *Hoax*

DESCRIPTIVE INCIDENT
DATE: *January 1978*
LOCATION: *Cononley, Yorkshire, England*
WITNESSES: *Tony Dodd, Alan Dale, and an unnamed policeman*

Sergeant Tony Dodd and Police Constable Alan Dale were driving down a pitch-dark country lane near Cononley one night when the road in front of them suddenly lit up bright as day. The officers stopped the car to investigate and, looking up, saw a bright object moving silently at about 40 mph just a hundred feet or so away from them. "The whole unit was glowing," Dodd recalled. "It was as if the metal of what this thing was made of was white hot."

As the object passed over their heads, Dodd and Dale saw that the saucer-shaped object had an elongated dome on top with portholes around it. At the bottom of the dome was a skirt with dazzling colored lights that danced around it, giving the impression that it was rotating. Under this "skirt" were three great spheres like huge ball bearings protruding below the object.

As the object moved on into the distance, it seemed to come down in a forest on the hillside to the officers' left. Dodd and Dale then continued on into town, until they crossed another police car coming the other way. When they stopped, the other police officer told them that he, too, had seen it.

The most surprising aspect of this sighting by U.K. policemen is that the craft they described sounds remarkably like the one seen—and photographed—a quarter century earlier by a rather dubious witness, the infamous contactee George Adamski. The infrequently reported UFO feature that Adamski first described are those three protruding spheres on the bottom of the domed saucer. Adamski twice managed to film and photograph this craft, which he called a Venusian scoutship, in 1952 and in 1965. But according to a photoanalysis conducted by the U.S. Air Force at Wright Patterson Air Force Base in Ohio, "these prints contain stimuli caused by a tobacco humidor and three ping pong balls."

While Adamski has been repeatedly ridiculed and denounced as a hoaxer, no one doubts the sincerity of Dodd and Dale. And the same distinctive feature continues to be reported in UFO sightings. A family hiking in Terra-Blugga National Park in Victoria, Australia, spotted just such a craft on May 2, 1998. The silver-gray disc with a large dome on top and three ball-like protrusions underneath hovered just 300 feet over their heads for about four minutes before taking off. Are all these people liars, or could Adamski's far-fetched experiences be real?

SOURCE: *Timothy Good,* Above Top Secret *(New York: Quill, 1988); Joseph Trainor (ed.), ''UFOs Remain Active All Around Australia,''* UFO Roundup, *3: 19, May 10, 1998.*

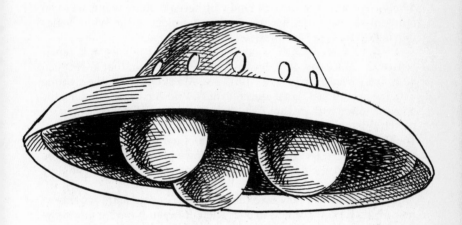

TYPE: *Discoid*
VARIANT: *Large domed disc*
SKEPTIC'S SOLUTION: *None*

DESCRIPTIVE INCIDENT

DATE: *July 28, 1989*
LOCATION: *Kapustin Yar, Astrakhan, Russia*
WITNESSES: *Ensign Valery N. Voloshin, Private Tishcahayev, Corporal Levin, Private Bashev, Private Kulik, Private Litvinov, First Lieutenant Klimenko*

One Soviet-era UFO case declassified by the KGB in 1991 involved a close encounter of the first kind with seven military witnesses at an army missile base that was the Soviet equivalent of the White Sands Proving Grounds in New Mexico.

At 11:20 that summer night a captain from the telegraph center alerted the officer on duty, Ensign Valery N. Voloshin, that a UFO had been flying over the base since 10:12 P.M. After confirming the sighting with the operational signal officer on duty, Voloshin began climbing the antenna tower with Private Tishcahayev, and immediately they saw "a powerful blinking signal which resembled a camera flash in the sky." The flashing light came from the bottom of a disc-shaped object, thirteen to seventeen feet in diameter, glowing a phosphorous green. Atop the disc was a large dome, which the witnesses described as a brightly lit half sphere.

At first the object flew over the base logistics yard and then moved toward the rocket weapons depot, where it began hovering just sixty-five feet off the ground. Suddenly "a bright beam appeared from the bottom of the disc, where the flash had been before, and made two or three circles, lighting the corner of one of the buildings." When the beam disappeared, the object moved on to the logistics yard, the railway station, and the cement factory, then back to the rocket depot, where it was also observed by the first guard shift and its commander.

First Lieutenant Klimenko reported that the object "accelerated abruptly and also stopped abruptly, all the while doing large jumps up or down." Two other objects then appeared in the distance, hovered for a while, then disappeared. At some point during the incident, an unspecified "command" called for a fighter intercept of the UFO. Klimenko reported that "the airplane, which could be identified by its noise, approached the object, but the object disengaged so fast that it seemed the plane stayed in place." The object evaded the fighter so quickly, in fact, that its pilot was unable to see the object in any detail.

The event ended more than three hours after the initial sighting, when, according to eyewitness depositions, the object flew toward Akhubinsk and disappeared at 1:30 in the morning.

SOURCE: *Don Berliner with Marie Galbraith and Antonio Huneeus,* Unidentified Flying Objects Briefing Document: The Best Available Evidence, *UFO Research Coalition, December 1995.*

TYPE: *Discoid*	**DESCRIPTIVE INCIDENT**
VARIANT: *Half disc*	DATE: *November 28, 1954*
SKEPTIC'S SOLUTION: *Unidentified*	LOCATION: *Manila, Philippines*
	WITNESSES: *Unnamed*

On this cool, clear night, a thirty-nine-year-old physician and former U.S. Army artillery officer with a B.A. in physics was in his automobile, driven by his chauffeur, traveling along Highway 54 south of Manila. At one point the doctor looked out the window and noticed a bright orange glow to the south. As the object approached, he told the chauffeur to stop the car and got out to get a better view of the object as it moved against a backdrop of high scattered clouds.

The glowing object traveled north for about three minutes then stopped, rising in elevation from 30 to 45 degrees in the process. Now the object was just 8,000 feet away. The doctor described it as being circular, with a dome-shaped top and a flat bottom. Though it glowed a bright orange color, it had four evenly spaced bright yellow "discs" or portholes along its side with a portion of the fifth visible at the edge. The object appeared flecked with red streaks and measured about seventy feet in diameter and twenty feet high. At no time did it make any sound.

A minute later the object began moving south, then reversed direction suddenly and resumed its original northerly course, disappearing in just three seconds. It left behind a bright orange-yellow exhaust trail. The chauffeur, who understood very little English, only caught sight of the object as it dashed away. This sighting is listed as one of the 701 unidentified cases in Project Blue Book files.

SOURCE: *Thomas M. Olson, (ed.),* The Reference for Outstanding UFO Sighting Reports *(Riderwood, MD: UFO Information Retrieval Center, Inc., 1966).*

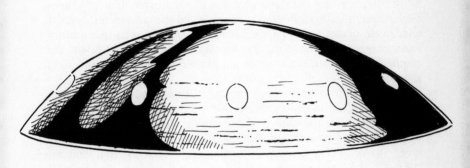

TYPE: *Discoid*	DESCRIPTIVE INCIDENT
VARIANT: *Disc with top "spikes"*	DATE: *September 29, 1995*
SKEPTIC'S SOLUTION: *None*	LOCATION: *Vejle, Jutland, Denmark*
	WITNESS: *Anonymous*

Driving alone at 9:30 at night in a remote wooded area near Vejle, a twenty-four-year-old Dane experienced car trouble. His speedometer suddenly shot to its highest reading, as did the tachometer, and the windshield blades began flapping madly to and fro, even though they hadn't been turned on. Next, his headlights dimmed, and finally the engine died altogether and he found himself stalled in the middle of the road.

He was still trying to restart the car when a dazzling light soundlessly "exploded" overhead. Opening the door, he had half exited the car when he saw the source of light ten to fifteen feet above him. Many separate beams of light, all described as rapidly blinking or quivering, streamed from a number of small bright "lamps" that were arranged in concentric circles on the bottom of the object. These circles of individual lights were spaced closer together as they approached the center of the disc, from which a small cluster of lights, or perhaps a single large light of the same sort—the area was too bright to make out any detail—shone straight down. Although not as blinding as an arc welder's light, the beams shared the same indigo tint. Moreover, instead of radiating or diffusing outward with distance, as a normal light might, they maintained their round, bar or tubelike shape all the way to the ground, so that the area illuminated exactly matched the circumference of the disc.

Slowly, the many brilliant beams diminished simultaneously in intensity, in the same way that household lights can now be dimmed in gradual degrees without having to be turned off all at once. At the same time, the disc began moving slowly forward, in the direction the car had been traveling before it stalled. Approaching a clump of nearby trees, the left side of the disc tipped up about twenty degrees to avoid colliding with them. Then, still in "dim" mode, the disc rapidly disappeared in the distance.

As the beam-emitting disc moved away, the driver was able to determine additional details. Its top outer edge was flared or very gently rounded, like a flattened parachute. Moreover, the top of the disc was studded with a series of spikes, or triangles, each of which was approximately a third of the object's overall diameter, or approximately ten feet tall.

SOURCE: *Kim Moeller Hansen, "Car Stop Encounter in Denmark" in* UFOs 1947–1997: Fifty Years of Flying Saucers, *Hilary Evans and Dennis Stacy, editors (London: John Brown Publishing, 1997).*

TYPE: *Discoid*	**DESCRIPTIVE INCIDENT**
VARIANT: *Disc with "legs"*	DATE: *January 1970*
SKEPTIC'S SOLUTION: *None*	LOCATION: *Tronstad, Norway*
	WITNESSES: *Ole Birkeland, Arne and Gudny Åsene, and others*

I t's rare for similar, unusually featured UFOs to be seen on consecutive nights by independent witnesses. But that's exactly what happened on two nights in January on Norway's southern coast. The first report came from a farmer and workshop employee named Ole Birkeland. At 9:30 that night, he was driving home across the moor to Tronstad, just northwest of Kristiansand, when he noticed a brightly lit object rising above the hill on the side of the road. To Birkeland's surprise, the object stopped suddenly, changed direction, and passed slowly in front of his car.

Birkeland described the object as looking like an illuminated baking tray with insectlike legs. Each of these seven "legs" ended in a knob that emitted a flame like a welding torch. The light from the object illuminated the area like a sports stadium. If the object made a sound, Birkeland could not hear it above the noise of his own car.

The strange object seemed to pursue Birkeland for about a mile or so, flying just 100 feet above his car. But as he neared Greipstad, the object headed off to the west, disappearing behind a hill. A Kristiansander driving the same route shortly after Birkeland saw a strong light over the moors, but no object.

The following evening, Arne and Gudny Åsene were driving over the Tronstad moor with their three children and a son-in-law when they encountered an intense light. After passing two cars that had stopped by the side of the road, they decided to pull over and investigate. Unaware of the Birkeland sighting, Arne and his son-in-law reported seeing a "cigar-shaped object with three lighted points" that sent a strong beam of light down onto the road.

The Åsenes then resumed their journey, with the object apparently following them off and on over a six mile stretch until they reached the Hoyle station on the southern railway. At that point the object was almost directly over them, about two hundred feet above the road. Suddenly the object began emitting flames, which seemed to melt the snow on either side of the road. Terrified, the Åsenes stopped their car under a railway bridge. Some minutes later the Åsenes continued on their way, the object still in pursuit for another couple of miles, before it finally disappeared when they reached Oyslebo.

All the witnesses remained silent about their experiences until reports of a sighting by a Danish policeman appeared in the press six months later.

SOURCE: *Richard Farrow, "Strange Object over Southern Norway,"* Flying Saucer Review Case Histories, *Supplement 4, April 1971.*

ELLIPTICAL
UFOs

TYPE: *Elliptical*
VARIANT: *Stretched "football"*
SKEPTIC'S SOLUTION: *Military aircraft*

DESCRIPTIVE INCIDENT

DATE: *October 28, 1975*
LOCATION: *Loring Air Force Base, Maine*
WITNESSES: *Clifton Blakeslee, Danny Lewis, William J. Long, Richard E. Chapman, Steven Eichner, R. Jones*

B etween October 27 and November 11, 1975, "suspicious unknown air activity" was reported by "reliable military personnel" at five NORAD (North American Aerospace Defense Command) bases from Maine to North Dakota, according to U.S. Defense Department documents. But of all the incidents, the one that took place at Loring Air Force Base on the second night of the "flap" seems most likely to involve an object that was truly out of the ordinary.

At 7:45 that night, Sgt. Clifton Blakeslee, Staff Sgt. William J. Long, and Sgt. Danny Lewis were on duty at the weapons storage area when they spotted what they at first thought were the running lights of an approaching aircraft. Following a call to the Command Post, Col. Richard E. Chapman, commander of the 42nd Bomber Wing, arrived and observed the mysterious object's flashing white and amber lights until 8:20 P.M. The object, which was picked up on radar as being three miles north of the base, behaved like a helicopter.

At one point the object shut off its lights, then reappeared about 150 feet over the flight line opposite the weapons storage area. Sgt. Steven Eichner, Sgt. R. Jones, and the rest of a B-52 crew working out of a "launch truck," then spotted the red and orange object, which was shaped, they said, like a "stretched-out football." The crew stared in awe as the object hovered, then turned off its lights, only to reappear moments later at the north end of the runway. The crew jumped into the truck and headed toward the object, which made jerky motions, then stopped once again.

Turning onto the road leading to the weapons storage area, the crew saw the object about three hundred feet ahead, hovering about five feet above the ground. The reddish-orange object was about four car lengths long. Crew chief Eichner reported seeing what looked like heat waves rising off the ground in front of it. "The object looked solid and we could not hear any noise coming from it," he noted. Neither could the crew see any doors, windows, propellers, engines, or other distinguishing features.

Suddenly, the base sirens began screaming. Police vehicles, blue lights flashing, came down the flight line toward the weapons storage area at high speed. Shortly afterward, the object shut off its lights and was not seen again that night. Radar tracked the object briefly, but lost it when it reached Grand Falls. A security sweep of the area turned up nothing.

The National Military Command Center and Chief of Staff of the Air Force were informed that an unknown object had penetrated the base and had been in the nuclear storage area that night. But some researchers believe that this and the other "NORAD flap" incidents were due to a covert exercise designed to test the military's intrusion detection and response capabilities.

SOURCE: *Lawrence Fawcett and Barry J. Greenwood,* Clear Intent: The Government's Coverup of the UFO Experience *(Englewood Cliffs, NJ: Prentice Hall, 1984).*

TYPE: *Elliptical*	**DESCRIPTIVE INCIDENT**
VARIANT: *Small domed "football"*	**DATE:** *March 20, 1966*
SKEPTIC'S SOLUTION: *Swamp gas*	**LOCATION:** *Dexter, Michigan*
	WITNESSES: *Frank Mannor, wife, and son Ronald, including two married daughters and their husbands, and numerous policemen*

The bang heard 'round the world, one of the most significant UFO sightings of all time, was first heard by six hunting dogs on the grounds of a farmhouse owned by Frank Mannor, a hunter, outdoorsman, and factory worker. When the dogs started "barkin' and bellerin' " at eight o'clock that Sunday night, Mannor ran from his house to see what all the commotion was about. Off to the east he saw a faint red glow, which he thought might be a fallen meteor—until it halted in midair before falling behind some trees in the distance. The entire family came out to see the reddish glow in the brush.

Mannor and his nineteen-year-old son then set out to investigate. When they got within five hundred yards of the glow, Mannor saw an object "the length of a car" and "shaped like a football" resting on a patch of haze about eight feet above the ground. A dome rose from the top of the object, and what looked like a pair of TV antenna rabbit ears stuck out from under its belly. A headlight seemed to be shining from the center of the object, while a red and white light rotated at one tip and a blue green light glimmered at the other. The object seemed metallic and quilted like a hand grenade. Then suddenly it turned a deep red and the lights went out. By the time Mannor and his son finally reached the place where the object had been, it was gone.

In the meantime, Mannor's wife had called the Dexter village police saying there was an object in the swamp that looked like a flying saucer. Police Chief Robert Taylor, Patrolman Nolan Lee, and Washtenaw County Deputy Stanley McFadden arrived in time to see a reddish light zipping over the Mannor farmhouse and giving off a sound "like an ambulance." Patrolman Robert Honeywell, who waited in the patrol car while the others went out, saw a strange, lighted object with red and white lights about a thousand feet high. He claimed the object swept over the swamps several times before being joined by three other objects and disappearing.

The following evening eighty-seven coeds and the assistant dean of women at Hillsdale College, about forty miles southwest of Dexter, observed a mysterious object outside their dormitory window. They, too, described a football-shaped object that wobbled, wavered, and glowed. The sightings created such a flurry of media interest that the Air Force dispatched astronomer J. Allen Hynek to investigate. By the end of the week Hynek had concluded that some of the Michigan sightings could be attributed to "swamp gas." But this explanation was widely ridiculed and politicians soon became involved, including then Michigan congressman (and later President) Gerald R. Ford, who called for congressional hearings. Held on April 6, 1966, these hearings eventually led the Air Force to sponsor a scientific investigation of the UFO phenomenon by the University of Colorado.

SOURCE: *Mort Young,* UFO: Top Secret *(New York: Essandess Special Edition, 1967).*

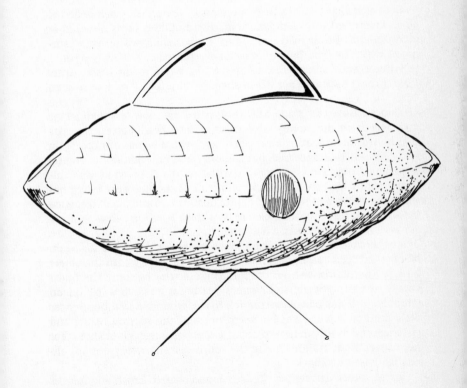

TYPE:	DESCRIPTIVE INCIDENT
Elliptical	DATE:
VARIANT:	*April 24, 1964*
Stretched "egg"	LOCATION:
SKEPTIC'S SOLUTION:	*Socorro, New Mexico*
Unidentified	WITNESS:
	Lonnie Zamora

At 5:45 P.M., Patrolman Lonnie Zamora broke off chasing a speeding car when he "heard a roar and saw a flame in the sky" descending behind a nearby hill, close to where he knew a dynamite shed to be situated. The blue, orange-tinged flame was shaped like an inverted cone or funnel, "narrower at the top than at the bottom."

Because of loose gravel, three attempts were necessary before he successfully crested the steep hill. Some two hundred yards away, in an arroyo slightly below road level, Zamora saw a shiny white, egg-shaped object which he first thought to be an overturned car. "Saw two people in white coveralls very close to object," he wrote in his report to the FBI. "[They] appeared normal in shape—but possibly they were small adults or large kids."

Zamora drove closer and parked his patrol car, now less than a hundred feet from the strange object. He radioed headquarters to report that he was investigating an accident and would be out of his car. The two figures had disappeared, but Zamora could now determine that the egg-shaped object was "smooth, [with] no doors or windows," and supported by legs. Moreover, in the middle of the side now facing him was a red insignia of some sort, approximately two and a half feet wide, consisting of three separate elements: a short baseline below an arrow shape, both overarched by a half circle.

At this point Zamora heard a low roar, and a flame similar to the one he had seen earlier began to emerge from underneath the object, blue in the main, with an orange fringe at the bottom. The object slowly rose straight up, and Zamora, fearing it was about to explode, stumbled into his patrol car and fell to the ground. Scrambling to his feet, he then put the car between him and the roaring object. The latter ascended to a height of about twenty-five feet, then shot off at high speed in a straight line to the southwest, narrowly missing the nearby dynamite shack.

Investigators visiting the site later found charred brush and four indentations in the sandy soil. These "landing traces" were arranged in the pattern of an asymmetrical diamond. After considerable investigation, the Air Force finally classified Zamora's sighting as "Unidentified."

SOURCE: *Kim Hansen "UFO Casebook,"* UFOs 1947–1997: The 40-Year Search for an Explanation, *compiled and edited by Hilary Evans with John Spencer (London: Fortean Tomes, 1987).*

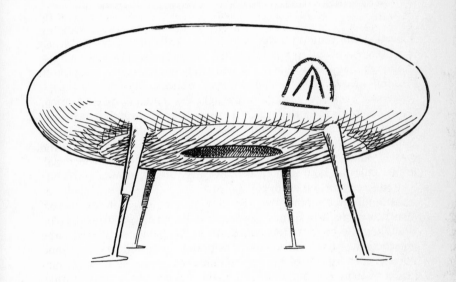

TYPE:	**DESCRIPTIVE INCIDENT**
Elliptical	**DATE:**
VARIANT:	*November 2, 1957*
Flat-bottomed oval	**LOCATION:**
SKEPTIC'S SOLUTION:	*Levelland, Texas*
Ball lightning	**WITNESSES:**
	Pedro Saucedo, Joe Salaz, Jim Wheeler, Jose Alvarez, Frank Williams, Sheriff Weir Clem, others

The first call came into the Levelland sheriff's office shortly before midnight—about an hour after the Soviet Union launched Sputnik II, though that news would not be widely known until later. In a pickup four miles west of Levelland, driver Pedro Saucedo, the caller, and passenger Joe Salaz saw a yellow-white light rise up out of a field to their right. According to Saucedo, it then "passed directly over the truck with a great sound and rush of wind." Saucedo also reported "a lot of heat" coming from the object, which he described as "torpedo-shaped, like a rocket," some two hundred feet long, and traveling at an estimated 600 to 800 miles an hour as it rushed away. As the object was overhead, Saucedo's engine and headlights failed.

An hour later another motorist, Jim Wheeler, called to say he had just encountered a brilliantly glowing egg-shaped object, 200 feet wide, straddling the highway four miles east of Levelland. As Wheeler approached the object, his engine stalled and his headlights went out. Wheeler stepped out of his car and watched as the object rose to a height of about two hundred feet and winked out. His car then started and ran normally.

At 12:05 A.M. a nineteen-year-old college freshman had his own lonely encounter, although it wouldn't be reported to the sheriff until the next day. He had been driving nine miles east of town when his engine sputtered and died and his headlights went out. He checked under the hood but could find nothing amiss. As he moved to return to the driver's seat, he became aware of an object sitting in the road ahead, glowing a bluish-green. He described it as oval-shaped, flat on the bottom, and approximately 125 feet long. He tried frantically, but in vain, to start the car. Finally, the object rose "almost straight up" and disappeared "in a split instant"—after which his car started normally.

At 12:15 A.M. yet another man called. He, too, had encountered a glowing object blocking the road, this time ten miles north of Levelland. As had happened to the college student, both his lights and engine died.

74

Again the object lifted vertically to a height of about three hundred feet, at which point its light went out and the man's car could be restarted.

At 12:45 A.M., truck driver Ronald Martin was just west of Levelland when his engine died after "a big ball of fire dropped on the highway." Martin said the object changed in color from red-orange to blue-green when it landed, then back to red-orange as it took off. The seventh and final call of the evening was from another truck driver, James Long, who also reported an egg-shaped object 200 feet long and glowing "like a neon sign."

At 1:30 in the morning, Sheriff Weir Clem and Deputy Pat McCulloch were about five miles outside of Levelland when they came across an oval-shaped light "looking like a brilliant red sunset across the highway."

SOURCE: *J. Allen Hynek, The UFO Experience: A Scientific Inquiry (Chicago: Henry Regnery Company, 1972); Ronald D. Story, UFOs and the Limits of Science (New York: William Morrow and Company, 1981).*

TYPE: *Elliptical*	**DESCRIPTIVE INCIDENT**
VARIANT: *Oval with tail appendage*	**DATE:** *October 10, 1966*
SKEPTIC'S SOLUTION: *Saturn*	**LOCATION:** *Newton, Illinois*
	WITNESSES: *Mrs. A and B, and five children*

Shortly before sunset, a rural housewife was called outside by her five children to see "the silent plane." Glimpsing out a south-facing window, her "first thought was that it was a plane making an emergency landing," as it was barely 35 feet off the ground.

Joining her children outdoors, "Mrs. A" watched the object as it continued on a leisurely westward trajectory. "It appeared to be larger than our car and more oval," she said. "There was a bluish glow around the ends, top, and bottom of it." The object itself was also a blue color and appeared to be made of metal; indeed, seam lines could be seen running its length. There was a single, black, rectangular window at the front of the object. Mrs. A had the feeling that "they (assuming someone was in it) could see out but we could not see them. I kept looking for someone to peep out and wave. . . ."

On the lower back end of the object, almost diagonally opposite the window, was what Mrs. A described as a "brownish-gold design," which she would later sketch for investigators. Atop this inscription or pattern, at the very end of the object, was a short tail or fin. "It moved quietly, making no sound at all except for a whirling or vibrating sound for one or two seconds as it drifted on toward the west. . . ."

Mrs. A and children watched apprehensively as the object approached some power lines running alongside a north-south gravel road, wondering whether it would be able to clear them. At the last moment it did "and was out of sight in just a few seconds." From start to finish the object had been in view for almost four minutes.

The case was investigated by Dr. George Kocher, an astronomer with the RAND Corporation, who was able to turn up a second independent witness, Mrs. B, who lived about seven miles away. (Both adult witnesses requested anonymity because of the possible reaction of friends and neighbors.) Kocher later estimated the length of the object at between sixteen and twenty feet, and its speed at between four and eight miles per hour, up until its final, abrupt departure.

SOURCE: *Karl T. Pflock, "UFOs: For RAND Use Only,"* The Anomalist 5, *Spring 1997.*

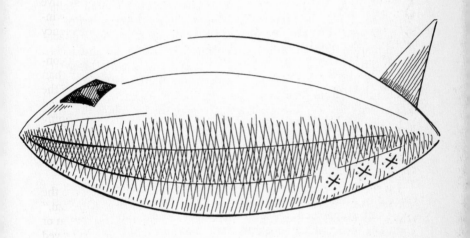

TYPE: *Elliptical*	**DESCRIPTIVE INCIDENT**
VARIANT: *Translucent "heel"*	**DATE:** *October 15, 1948*
SKEPTIC'S SOLUTION: *None*	**LOCATION:** *Kyushu, Japan*
	WITNESSES: *Oliver Hemphill Jr.,*
	Barton Halter

On this clear, moonlit night, an F-61 belonging to the 68th Fighter Squadron was on a routine mission off the northwest coast of Kyushu. The pilot was First Lieutenant Oliver Hemphill Jr.; Second Lieutenant Barton Halter was the radar operator. At 11:05 P.M. Halter picked up an airborne target five miles dead ahead and slightly below the F-61. When the target took no evasive action, Halter assumed it must be an aircraft from their home field. But before he knew it the target had passed the F-61, diving below it. The pilot tried to follow the target but it had disappeared from radar.

The target then reappeared up ahead, but after adding a burst of speed, the object quickly outdistanced the F-61 again. On the third interception, Hemphill and Halter spotted the object visually on their left. The pilot saw the object in silhouette against a very reflective overcast created by a full moon. He described it as a translucent object with a very short, stubby body, about the length of a conventional fighter aircraft. The object had a largely flat bottom, a rounded front, and a top surface that sloped down to its tail, which cut off sharply. The object had no wings, no tail, no canopy, no visible engines. "I realized at this time that it did not look like any type of aircraft I was familiar with," Hemphill noted. When the pilot contacted Ground Control, he learned they had no other aircraft in the area; nor did the UFO show up on their radar.

Hemphill then tried to pull ahead of the object, but just as they got astern of it, the object took off in a burst of speed, disappearing off the radar scope nine or ten miles away. On the fourth encounter, the pilot got a fleeting glance of the object as it passed the F-61 from behind and above, then disappeared off radar five to ten miles ahead. On the fifth and sixth interceptions, the target appeared on the screen as being nine miles ahead, but each time it quickly pulled away beyond the F-61's airborne radar range of ten miles.

"Intelligence reports from Far East air forces indicated that the UFOs might have 'carried radar warning equipment,' because the 'object seemed cognizant of the whereabouts of the F-61 at all times,' " according to astronomer J. Allen Hynek, consultant to the Air Force's Project Blue Book. The Kyushu case puzzled Project Grudge, a Blue Book predecessor and the Air Force's second attempt to investigate UFOs, which classified it "Unidentified."

SOURCE: *J. Allen Hynek,* The Hynek UFO Report *(New York: Dell, 1977).*

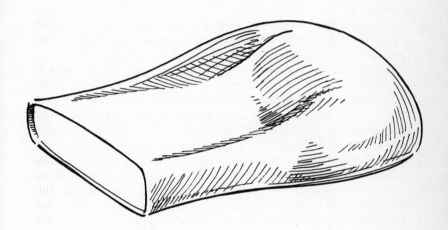

TYPE: *Elliptical*	**DESCRIPTIVE INCIDENT**
VARIANT: *Egg on column*	**DATE:** *January 20, 1988*
SKEPTIC'S SOLUTION: *Meteorite fall*	**LOCATION:** *Mundrabilla, Australia*
	WITNESSES: *Faye, Patrick, Sean, and Wayne Knowles, Graham Henley*

During the Australian bicentennial, Faye Knowles and her three sons left their home in Perth for a holiday in Melbourne. At about four o'clock in the morning the foursome were driving along the Erie Highway in Australia's southwestern desert when they noticed a strange light up ahead. The closer they got to the object, the bigger and brighter it appeared.

Sean, twenty-one, who was driving at the time, thought it looked like a "spaceship." The family would later describe the shape of this white object as "an egg in an egg cup," or an oval on top of a tapered column that reached down to the ground. In the center of the egg was a yellow light.

Eventually the object loomed so large that it blocked their view of the road, and Sean swerved to avoid hitting it, nearly colliding with a station wagon headed the opposite way as he did so. He then made several U-turns in pursuit of the object, but the family lost sight of it. Suddenly, they heard a thump and thought the object had landed on the roof of their car. The family felt as if the car was lifted into the air, but no one remembered seeing anything protruding from the car top, nor did anyone recall looking out the window and viewing the road below while the car was supposedly suspended in the air.

The Knowles family later reported a series of events that occurred in an indeterminate sequence. They heard a humming sound. Their voices changed in pitch and appeared to slow down. Their two dogs went crazy. And the whole family became hysterical, shouting, crying, and thinking they were going to die.

Sometime later the object dropped the car back down onto the ground, bursting the left rear tire in the process. Sean quickly applied the brakes and brought the car to a stop. He then blacked out momentarily. Meanwhile, when Faye Knowles, forty-eight, rolled down her window, the car filled with a grayish-black smoke. Frightened, the family then fled the vehicle, scrambling into some roadside bushes until the object departed. From the moment they first spotted the light, their "reign of terror," as it was called, had lasted about an hour and a half.

The family then changed the tire on the car and drove to a truck stop in Mundrabilla. There they encountered a truck driver named Graham Henley who said he had seen a strange light behind him on the same road. He described it as very bright and like "a big fried egg hung upside down." The Knowles family then traveled on to Ceduna, where they reported the incident to the police.

SOURCE: *Keith Basterfield,* "The Mundrabilla Incident—January 20th, 1988, Investigation Report," *The Fund for UFO Research (Mt. Rainier, Maryland: November 1988).*

CYLINDRICAL UFOs

TYPE: *Cylindrical*
VARIANT: *Flying "immigrant wagon"*
SKEPTIC'S SOLUTION: *None*

DESCRIPTIVE INCIDENT
DATE: *April 13, 1897*
LOCATION: *St. Elmo, Minnesota*
WITNESSES: *Frederick Chamberlain and two others*

The year 1897 saw a wave of mystery airships reported across the United States. These objects were generally described as cigar-shaped, apparently metallic, and often bearing wings, propellers, fins, and bright lights at night. While the British and the French were known to have motor-powered balloons at the time, aviation historians insist that no such craft was in operation in the United States in the 1890s. (The first dirigible flew in 1900—in Germany.) The situation was muddied both by practical jokers, who sent all kinds of balloons aloft, and by enterprising newspaper reporters who delighted in making up tall airship tales for publication. But some UFOs of the modern variety were observed at the time, one of the most credible being a craft that landed briefly in a field in Minnesota.

On the night in question, Frederick Chamberlain and his companion were riding to Hudson. At 11:00 P.M. they spotted a figure walking around in a clearing "as if he were looking for something," noted Chamberlain. As the two men turned off the road to investigate, they heard a crackling sound followed by an irregular "rushing noise," according to a news article that appeared in the *St. Paul Pioneer Press* of April 15.

Then suddenly they beheld ahead of them a long, high object of a gray-white color. "The thing struck me as resembling most of the top of a 'prairie schooner' or immigrant wagon covered with canvas," said Chamberlain. The object had two rows of lights on it, four lights in two pairs, one red and the other green.

Without warning the object rose at an angle, barely clearing the tree-tops. As it headed south, the two men saw some additional white lights on the object, which, they noted, had no wings, wheels, machinery, or human figures visible on it. At about the same time, a farmer living nearby reported seeing an object with red and green lights fly over the area.

When Chamberlain and his companion went to examine the place where the object had rested on the ground, they found, in the mud, "fourteen footprints . . . each two feet in length, six inches wide, arranged seven on each side, and in an oblong pattern."

SOURCE: *Jerome Clark*, The Emergence of A Phenomenon: UFOs from the Beginning through 1959 *(Detroit: Omnigraphics, 1992).*

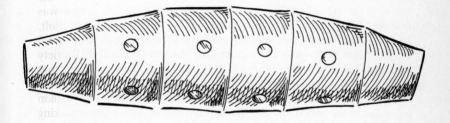

TYPE: *Cylindrical*	**DESCRIPTIVE INCIDENT**
VARIANT: *"Cigar" with lights*	**DATE:** *May 25, 1995*
SKEPTIC'S SOLUTION: *None*	**LOCATION:** *Bovina, Texas*
	WITNESSES: *Eugene Tollefson, John J. Waller, and an unnamed flight attendant*

America West Flight 564 from Tampa, Florida, to Las Vegas was crossing the Texas panhandle into New Mexico at an altitude of 39,000 feet, when a flight attendant sitting in the jump seat behind the copilot noticed something out the right window. The co-pilot, First Officer John J. Waller, turned and saw, at the three o'clock position, a row of flashing lights to the left of an isolated thunderstorm cell. It looked to him like "eight strobes in a line" with the outer lights flashing continuously, while the other six went on and off sequentially from left to right.

The flight attendant saw it somewhat differently. He described the leftmost light flashing, followed by "a beam of light or a series of smaller lights or a reflection" traveling to the right where the outer light then flashed on. The pilot, Captain Eugene Tollesfson, who had to stand to see past the others, recalled seeing intense lights at each end with smaller white lights in between.

Waller immediately contacted the Albuquerque Air Route Traffic Control Center, but the object was not showing up on their radar screens. The controller then called Cannon Air Force Base in Clovis, New Mexico, and learned that there were no military operations in progress.

As the flight continued, the UFO eventually appeared in front of, and about half way in between, the towering thundercloud forty-five miles away. Now, as the lightning flashed, the witnesses could clearly discern that the mystery lights were located on a wingless, "cigar-shaped" silhouette of "unbelievable" length; Waller estimated it was 300 to 400 feet long. Tollesfson, who got "two good looks" at the object, thought it was even larger, perhaps 400 to 500 feet across. He also noted that the silhouette was slightly curved above and below the lights.

An eastbound military aircraft, identified as "Hawk 85," did report something "a little lower than us off our left wing" without going into any further detail, but no other aircraft in the area reported seeing anything unusual. A call from air traffic controllers to NORAD revealed an unidentified track at 11:02 P.M., but six minutes later it was shown to be a known aircraft. In a follow-up call to NORAD the next day, however, the controller learned that they had detected another target in the area, "which appeared stationary at first, then accelerated suddenly for twenty to thirty seconds, and came to an abrupt stop again. Over a period of about four minutes the object had repeatedly accelerated up to speeds of 1,000 to 1,400 mph and stopped. An investigation revealed no prosaic explanation for the sighting.

SOURCE: *Walter N. Webb,* Final Report on the America West Airline Case—May 25–26, 1995 *(Washington, DC: UFO Research Coalition, 1997).*

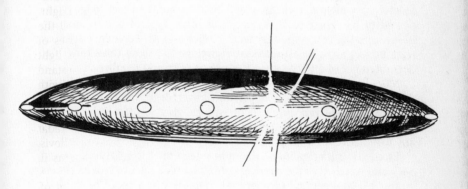

TYPE: *Cylindrical*
VARIANT: *"Torpedo" with windows*
SKEPTIC'S SOLUTION: *Meteor*

DESCRIPTIVE INCIDENT
DATE: *July 24, 1948*
LOCATION: *Montgomery, Alabama*
WITNESSES: *Capt. Clarence S. Chiles, John B. Whitted, Clarence L. McKelvie*

The Eastern Airlines DC-3 out of Houston, bound for Atlanta and flying at 5,000 feet, was twenty miles southwest of Montgomery, Alabama, when history happened. Captain Chiles was at the controls, Whitted was co-pilot. At 2:45 A.M., alarmed by a rapidly closing light, Chiles tapped Whitted on the arm, pointed, and pulled the plane into a tight left turn.

Off to the right, barely 700 feet away, the light blazed by. Both pilots reported a wingless, torpedo shape about a hundred feet long. It appeared to be "powered by some jet or other type of power shooting flame from the rear some fifty feet," Chiles told Air Force investigators from Project Sign. He estimated the fuselage as "about three times the circumference of a B-29," then the country's largest bomber.

Moreover, said Chiles, "there were two rows of [large square] windows, which indicated an upper and lower deck, [and] from inside these windows a very bright light was glowing. Underneath the ship there was a blue glow of light . . . We heard no noise nor did we feel any turbulence from the object."

From his vantage point on the right side of the DC-3, Whitted looked back and watched as the streaking object banked up into broken clouds at about 6,000 feet and disappeared from view at a speed of approximately 700 mph. From beginning to end the incident had lasted not less than five seconds nor more than ten.

Because of the hour, only one passenger aboard the plane, Clarence L. McKelvie of Columbus, Ohio, saw the object, and then only as "this strange eerie streak . . . I could not get my eyes adjusted to it before it was gone." McKelvie added that "it was very intense, not like lightning or anything I had ever seen."

SOURCE: *Jerome Clark,* The UFO Book *(Detroit: Visible Ink Press, 1998), pp. 77–79.*

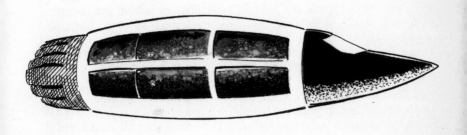

TYPE: *Cylindrical*
VARIANT: *"Cigar" with dome*
SKEPTIC'S SOLUTION: *Meteor*

DESCRIPTIVE INCIDENT

DATE: *October 18, 1973*
LOCATION: *Mansfield, Ohio*
WITNESSES: *Captain Lawrence Coyne, Arrigo Jezzi, John Healey, Robert Yanacsek*

In the midst of the great UFO wave that engulfed the United States that October, the crew of an Army helicopter experienced something that believers and critics alike agree was out-of-this-world. It was a clear, cool night when the Army Reserve UH-1 Huey helicopter left Columbus for its base back in Cleveland. From his rear seat, John Healey, a Cleveland policeman who was the flight medic, was the first to notice a steady southbound red light that disappeared behind the chopper. Then a couple of minutes later Sergeant Robert Yanacsek, the crew chief, saw a bright red light on the eastern horizon that seemed to be keeping pace with them. He mentioned it to Captain Lawrence Coyne, who told him to keep an eye on it.

Thirty seconds later Yanacsek reported that the light was coming toward the helicopter, and Coyne took the controls from First Lieutenant Arrigo Jezzi, putting the helicopter into a normal descent. As he did so, Coyne called Mansfield Approach Control on the radio and asked if there were any high performance craft in the area. After initial radio acknowledgment, radio contact failed on both UHF and VHF frequencies.

As the red light continued to close in on them at an alarming rate, Coyne sent the chopper into a dive. When it got to within 650 feet above the treetops, the captain looked up to see that the object had *stopped* just above and in front of the helicopter. There, clearly delineated against the background stars, was a cigar-shaped, gray metallic object with a slight dome on top. Yanacsek thought he saw some windows along this upper dome. The object, which basically filled the entire front windshield of the helicopter, had a red light on its nose and a white light at the other end. But the witnesses could see no wings, tail, or identifying marks on the well-lit object.

From underneath the object's stern a green, pyramid-shaped beam swept a ninety-degree arc and shone through the helicopter windshield, bathing the cockpit in a green light. The object hovered over the helicopter like this for about ten seconds before accelerating and heading off toward the northwest. After a sharp forty-five-degree turn to the right, the white light snapped out over the horizon. At that point Coyne noted that though his control stick was still down from his descent, the helicopter was actually climbing at 1,000 feet per minute.

Other witnesses were later found to have seen the encounter from the ground. But UFO skeptic Philip Klass argued that the crew had seen nothing more than a meteor or fireball from the Orionids meteor shower. While meteors do not last more than a few seconds, this encounter had lasted five minutes from start to finish.

SOURCE: *Jennie Zeidman,* A Helicopter-UFO Encounter Over Ohio *(Evanston, Illinois: Center for UFO Studies, 1979).*

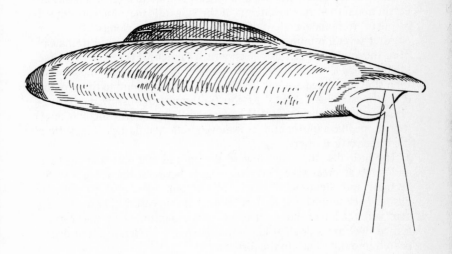

TYPE: *Cylindrical*
VARIANT: *"Cloud cigar"*
SKEPTIC'S SOLUTION: *None*

DESCRIPTIVE INCIDENT
DATE: *September 14, 1954*
LOCATION: *Vendée, France*
WITNESSES: *Georges Fortin, Louis Grellier, Madame Pizou, and others*

A storm was brewing at five o'clock in the afternoon, as thirty-four-year-old Georges Fortin worked in the fields of his farm with his men. Suddenly, a luminous blue mist, shaped like a "carrot," emerged from the thick layer of storm clouds. Fortin, his men, and farmers all over the countryside watched intently as this rigid "cloud" descended rapidly from the cloud ceiling in a horizontal position slightly tilted toward the ground "like a submerging submarine." Half a mile above their heads the object stopped and quickly shifted to a vertical position. Fortin noted that the movements of the "gigantic machine surrounded by mists" were independent of the movement of the clouds.

After several minutes a white, vaporlike smoke began to trail away from the lower end of this object, which French UFO researcher Aimé Michel called a "cloud cigar." This "smoke" first fell toward the ground, then slowed, turned around, and began to spiral around to the very top of the mysterious "cloud." As the trail gradually dissolved, the witnesses could see the object that had "sowed" it—"a little metallic disc" that shone like a mirror and, as it moved, reflected flashes of light from the huge vertical object.

The little disc then shot toward the ground and darted about back and forth at great speed over the region between the villages of St. Prouant and Sigournais, located about four miles apart. Finally, it dashed back to the large vertical "cloud," disappearing "like a shooting star" into the lower end of the object. About a minute later the "carrot" leaned over to its original horizontal position, accelerated, and disappeared into the clouds in the distance.

Fortin's account was corroborated by Louis Grellier, his thirty-six-year-old farmhand, who independently gave an identical account of the sighting, and Madame Pizou, a sixty-seven-year-old widow who was working in a cabbage field about a mile away. With Pizou were her daughter and a farmhand who also confirmed the object's maneuvers, aerial designs by the smoke trail, and half hour duration of the sighting. In all, several hundred people witnessed this extraordinary event.

SOURCE: *Aimé Michel,* Flying Saucers and the Straight Line Mystery *(New York: Criterion Books, 1958).*

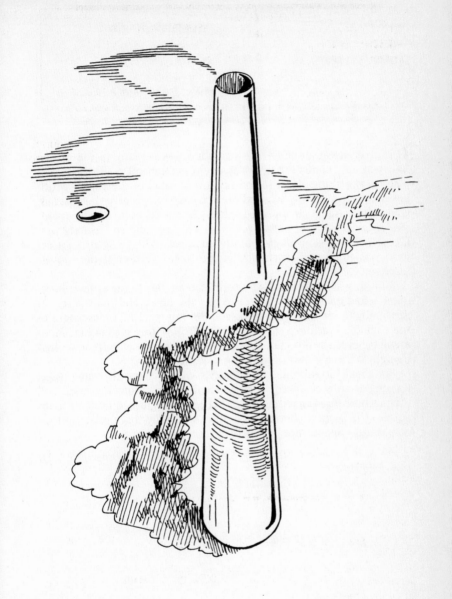

TYPE: *Cylindrical*
VARIANT: *"Spindle"*
SKEPTIC'S SOLUTION: *None*

DESCRIPTIVE INCIDENT
DATE: *Summer 1930*
LOCATION: *Pietermaritzburg, Natal, South Africa*
WITNESSES: *A. M. Richmond and "Comprehend"*

On a very clear summer day Richmond was working in the garden when the family's native servant, Comprehend, called out and pointed to a shiny object in the sky. Every detail of the object, which hovered over a heavily wooded area beyond the property boundaries, was plainly visible. "It appeared to me," Richmond wrote, "to be a massive sheet of shining metal, revolving on a spindle so leisurely that I expected it to stop rotating at any moment. With each turn a great flash was thrown off each side of the 'sheet' section of the spindle machine. . . ."

Since it was so rare to even observe an aircraft in those days, Richmond's first inclination was to run into the house and call the rest of the family to see this unusual object. But not wanting to lose sight of the "spindle machine," the witness overcame this inclination. Richmond believed the object might be from another planet, but the servant thought it was a visitor from the land of the spirits.

For about forty minutes the object stayed in about the same place, rotating at an even speed. Then suddenly the rotations increased and the machine lifted up at incredible speed "as if plucked by some giant hand." The flashes followed each other so rapidly that the object took on a starlike appearance. It was then soon lost to sight.

SOURCE: *A. M. Richmond, "The Flying Spindle,"* Flying Saucer Review, *16(3) 21, May–June 1970.*

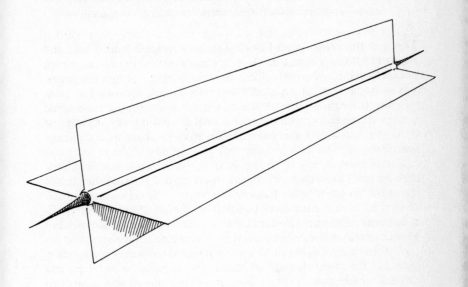

TYPE: *Cylindrical*	**DESCRIPTIVE INCIDENT**
VARIANT: *"Bullet" with fin*	**DATE:** *February 25, 1951*
SKEPTIC'S SOLUTION: *None*	**LOCATION:** *Mount Kilimanjaro, Tanzania*
	WITNESSES: *Jack Bicknell, Dennis Merrifield, H. B. Fussell, and eight others*

The Lodestar plane, piloted by Captain Jack Bicknell, left Nairobi airport at 7:00 on a clear and cloud-free morning. Twenty minutes later Dennis Merrifield, the radio officer, drew Bicknell's attention to a bright white star hanging about 10,000 feet over Mount Kilimanjaro. After watching it for three minutes, the crew decided to alert the passengers.

Over the next fourteen minutes a total of eleven people would see the mysterious object and later sign an affidavit about their sighting. Two of the passengers reportedly took photographs of the object. Captain H. B. Fussell, one of the passengers, immediately pulled out his high-powered binoculars and began observing it. "Through the glasses the object appeared bullet-shaped," he noted. "The color was whitish-silver with three vertical black bands down the side."

Meanwhile, as the Lodestar held its course, Bicknell raised Eastleigh Tower by radio and reported what they were seeing. Eastleigh asked the crew if the object might not be a meteorological balloon. The pilot then looked at the object through binoculars. What he saw was "definitely metallic," more than 200 feet long, and bullet-shaped with a square-cut vertical fin at one end. The object was a dull silver color with black bands at regular intervals along the fuselage. Its outline was not hazy, but "clear and sharp," according to Bicknell.

The object remained stationary for another ten minutes, then rose suddenly, gaining another 5,000 feet. After being motionless for about a minute, it rose again, to 40,000 feet, then moved away eastward "at a terrific speed."

SOURCE: Cynthia Hind, UFOs Over Africa *(Madison, Wisconsin: Horus House, 1997).*

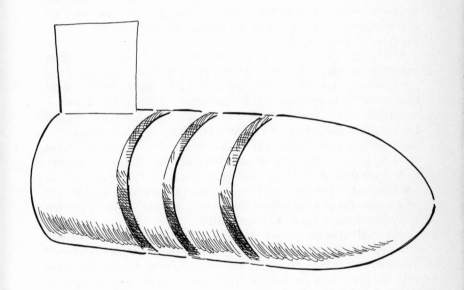

TYPE: *Cylindrical*
VARIANT: *"Drum"*
SKEPTIC'S SOLUTION: *Jupiter and perhaps Mars*

DESCRIPTIVE INCIDENT
DATE: *November 17, 1986*
LOCATION: *Fort Yukon, Alaska*
WITNESSES: *Kenju Terauchi, Takanori Tamefuji, Yoshio Tsukuba*

Japan Airlines Flight 1628 was flying from Paris to Tokyo via Reykjavik, Iceland, and Anchorage, Alaska, with a cargo of Beaujolais nouveau. At 5:11 P.M., as the Boeing 747 freighter was passing over northeastern Alaska, Captain Kenju Terauchi noticed some lights about 2,000 feet below on his left.

The lights seemed to travel with the plane for several minutes, when suddenly "two spaceships stopped in front of our face," as Captain Terauchi would later tell FAA investigators. Each "spaceship" consisted of a pair of nearly rectangular arrays of light, separated by a narrow rectangular dark area in between. Terauchi's later drawing of the objects suggests the light arrays actually lay on a cylindrical surface. The lights seemed to be produced by amber and white flames coming out of multiple exhaust ports. The co-pilot, Takanori Tamefuji, found the objects "very strange" because there were "too many lights" and "it was too luminous." The flight engineer, Yoshio Tsukuba, also saw the light arrays from his position behind the co-pilot, and like the others, he too described the light clusters as "undulating."

Tamefuji called Anchorage flight control to try to find out what was going on, but they were unable to correlate the two "aircraft" a mile ahead of JAL 1628 with any known traffic. After moving in formation with the plane for a few minutes, the objects abruptly rearranged their orientation from one over the other to side by side. Captain Terauchi then attempted to take a photograph of the objects, but his camera failed to work properly. The crew also experienced a good deal of interference in their radio contact with flight control while the strange objects stayed close to the airplane.

Twelve minutes into the event, the JAL crew reported that the lights on the objects suddenly "extinguished." Terauchi believed they flew away, leaving behind a "pale white flat light" to his left. When the pilot decided to see if he could pick up anything on his radar, he found a weak target located seven to eight miles away in the ten o'clock position. The Elmendorf Regional Operational Control Center also picked up an unidentified "surge primary return" on their radar, but only for about a minute.

Twenty minutes into the event, the captain checked to see what had happened to the pale white light behind them, and saw "the silhouette of a gigantic spaceship." He described the Saturn-shaped object as being about the size of an aircraft carrier. Frightened, Terauchi immediately requested course and altitude change in an attempt to evade the object. During a subsequent 360-degree turn, military radar picked up something behind the freighter, and flight control asked Terauchi if he wanted "a scramble on the traffic." But the pilot turned down the offer, not wanting to endanger anyone else. Flight control then asked a United Airlines flight in the vicinity to confirm the presence of unknown traffic behind JAL 1628. But when the United flight came side by side, Terauchi recalled, the spaceship suddenly disappeared. The United pilot never saw anything near JAL 1628.

A follow-up FAA investigation concluded that the radar records could not confirm the event because the returns reported by the controller were thought to be an artifact of the radar set. But UFO skeptic Philip Klass and the Committee for Investigation of Claims of the Paranormal issued a press release saying that the JAL crew had been fooled by the planets Jupiter and, probably, Mars. While the giant spaceship seen by the captain behind the plane might be dismissed as an overexcited misinterpretation of oddly lit clouds, the arrays of lights observed by the entire crew directly in front of the plane remain unexplained.

SOURCE: *Bruce Maccabee,* The Fantastic Flight of JAL 1628 *(Mt. Rainier, MD: Fund for UFO Research, 1987).*

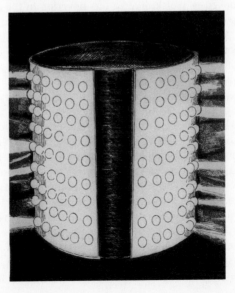

TYPE: *Cylindrical*
VARIANT: *Rectangular cylinder*
SKEPTIC'S SOLUTION: *None*

DESCRIPTIVE INCIDENT
DATE: *May 10, 1978*
LOCATION: *Emilcin, Poland*
WITNESSES: *Jan Wolski and a young boy*

Jan Wolski, a seventy-one-year-old farmer, lived in a small agricultural hamlet in eastern Poland. On the day of the incident, he had left his farm at five in the morning in a wagon drawn by a young mare. Some two hours later he passed two people walking in his direction along a country road and was struck not only by the way they walked—performing supple jumps like divers on the seabed—but also by the curious greenish tint of their faces. Suddenly the two "freaks," as Wolski called them, jumped into his wagon, one on each side of him. He noticed how strange their clothes were: their one-piece overalls ended in some kind of foot flipper. Wolski thought they were "foreigners" because they had slanted eyes, prominent cheekbones, and spoke in an incomprehensible language that sounded to him like "ta-ta-ta-ta."

Wolski nonchalantly took it in stride until a short while later, as the wagon traveled on, they came across a strange vehicle in a clearing near a dense wall of trees. The rectangular-shaped vehicle with its slightly curved roof looked to Wolski like "a bus hovering in the air." Hanging below the top of the nearby birches, the object looked to be about ten feet wide, fifteen feet long, and less than ten feet high (other sources have it as about thirty feet long and more than twelve feet high). At each corner of the object was a barrel-shaped something mounted on quickly rotating "screws" that emitted a buzzing sound.

The humanoids then signaled Wolski to step on a platform that was lowered from the object. Wolski did so, then rose up into a dark rectangular room, where he met two more "foreigners," who told him to remove his clothes. After a brief examination with "two plates," he was told to get dressed. He then took the platform down, got in his wagon, and galloped the rest of the way home. After telling his sons what had happened, they returned to the clearing and found a series of "trapezoidal, almost rectangular" footprints. Investigators later located a six-year-old boy nearby who had seen an aircraft resembling a bus flying very low over their barn. The object, the boy said, then climbed vertically into the air and vanished.

Psychologists, sociologists, and physicians from the University of Lodz who examined and questioned Wolski and looked into his background were convinced he was telling the truth. "I solemnly swear by God that my account about the encounter with extraterrestrials on 10 May 1978, is absolutely true," Wolski's signed oath states. "God is my witness that I am telling the truth." UFO investigators regard the Wolski case a benchmark abduction account, with little or no contamination from the outside world and none of the media exposure that characterizes American abduction stories.

SOURCE: Antonio Huneeus, "UFO Chronicle, The Wolski Case: A Polish Abduction," Fate, September 1994.

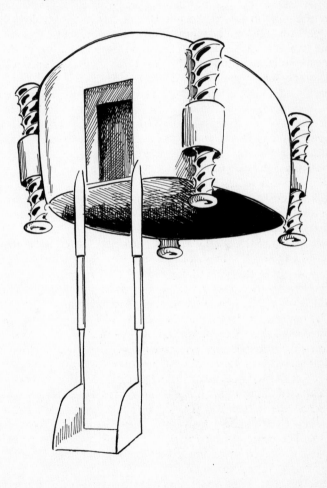

RECTANGULAR
UFOs

TYPE: *Rectangular*	**DESCRIPTIVE INCIDENT**
VARIANT: *"Cushion"*	DATE: *November 22, 1966*
SKEPTIC'S SOLUTION: *None*	LOCATION: *New York, New York*
	WITNESSES: *D. R. McVay, W. H. Leick,*
	A. A. LaSalle, and five others

Sometimes, even when the news might fit, no one has any interest in printing it. That's what at least eight employees of the American Newspaper Publishers Association (ANPA) discovered after spotting a UFO over one of the world's largest cities on a bright sunny day in the fall of 1966.

From their offices on the seventeenth floor of 750 Third Avenue, D. R. McVay, the assistant general manager of the ANPA, and the other witnesses were treated to a truly unusual sight, even by New York City standards. What they saw was a rectangular, cushion-shaped object, heading south over the East River at 4:20 in the afternoon. The object then stopped and hovered over the United Nations building, or so it appeared, for several minutes. As it fluttered and bobbed like a ship in rough seas, the object reflected the sun's light with a golden glint. When the object departed, it rose upward rapidly, then headed east, also at high speed.

James E. McDonald, a senior physicist with the Institute of Atmospheric Physics at the University of Arizona in Tucson, became interested in the case and spoke to one of the witnesses. W. H. Leick told McDonald that they had called the Air Force, which promised to send an officer over the next day to interview them, but no one ever did. And when the witnesses phoned a New York City newspaper, the "unnamed" paper said it was not interested. The report finally reached the National Investigations Committee on Aerial Phenomenon (NICAP), a private UFO group that achieved high visibility during the 1960s. They sent the witnesses questionnaires to fill out and published a report on the case in the January–February 1967 issue of the NICAP newsletter, *The UFO Investigator.*

"I accept this as a quite real sighting, made by reliable observers under viewing circumstances that would seem to rule out obvious conventional explanations," McDonald noted in a statement he prepared for a Congressional hearing on UFOs held on July 29, 1968. He used the case to rebut skeptics who asked: Why aren't UFOs ever seen in cities?

SOURCE: *James E. McDonald, "Prepared Statement on Unidentified Flying Objects," Symposium on Unidentified Flying Objects, Hearing Before the Committee on Science and Aeronautics, U.S. House of Representatives, Ninetieth Congress, July 29, 1968 (Washington, DC: U.S. Government Printing Office, 1968).*

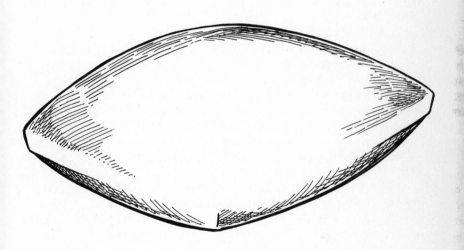

TRIANGULAR
UFOs

TYPE: *Triangular*	**DESCRIPTIVE INCIDENT**
VARIANT: *"Beehive"*	DATE: *December 21, 1964*
SKEPTIC'S SOLUTION: *Psychological*	LOCATION: *Fisherville, Virginia*
	WITNESSES: *Horace Burns and one unnamed boy*

Despite popular lore, few UFOs turn out to be "hot" in a radioactive sense. But one that may have been made a brief appearance in the western portion of Virginia just a few days before Christmas of 1964. At five o'clock in the afternoon Horace Burns, a gunsmith, was heading east on Route 250 and approaching Fisherville when an immense object slowly crossed low over the highway ahead of him. The object was so large and so close that it filled the entire windshield of his car. As it descended, the object narrowly missed the nearby power lines and settled "like a bubble" into a meadow off to the right of the highway.

Quite suddenly, Burns's engine died, but he managed to pull the car off on the shoulder before it came to a complete stop. He then stepped out into the gathering darkness to better see the remarkable object just a hundred yards away. It was shaped somewhat like a beehive. From a circular base about 125 feet in diameter, the sides of the object sloped up to the top in six concentric convolutions that gradually decreased in diameter, the last and smallest forming a dome on top.

The object had a dull metallic finish and was essentially featureless—no windows, doors, ports, seams, or even landing gear. Its somewhat convex underside seemed to rest directly on the ground. It was eighty to ninety feet tall, and illuminated from a sharply edged, twelve to eighteen-inch band of bluish-white light located about six feet up from its base.

After a minute or so the object rose straight up several hundred feet, emitted a soft whooshing sound, and shot off rapidly toward the northeast. Within seconds it was out of sight. Burns then got back in his car, which started without a problem, and drove home. At first he only told his wife what had happened, but six days later, after hearing that a small group of people at nearby Eastern Mennonite College had decided to investigate UFOs he agreed to tell his story to the group's leader, a professor of German named Ernest Gehman.

On December thirtieth, Burns was supposed to show Gehman the landing spot, but he could not leave the gun shop. With only minimal directions from Burns, however, Gehman found the exact location of the encounter because the needle on the Geiger counter he had brought along went off the scale. Two Dupont engineers who joined Gehman at the site verified the high readings. While Air Force investigators subsequently discounted the high Geiger counter returns, they did not think that Burns was a hoaxer. Nonetheless, the Air Force wrote off the Burns case as "psychological" in origin, unaware that a fourteen-year-old boy had independently seen the same object from his home in Staunton at 4:50 P.M. that day.

SOURCE: *Jerome Clark*, High Strangeness: UFOs from 1960 through 1979 *(Detroit: Omnigraphics, 1996), pp. 202–206.*

TYPE: *Triangular*	**DESCRIPTIVE INCIDENT**
VARIANT: *Faceted cone*	DATE: *October 5, 1996*
SKEPTIC'S SOLUTION: *None*	LOCATION: *Pelotas, Brazil*
	WITNESS: *Haraldo Westendorf*

B razil has always been a hotbed of sensational UFO stories. This incident, which took place in broad daylight, is tame only by comparison. On this Saturday morning, Haraldo Westendorf, a forty-year-old businessman, would fly his single-engine Piper Apache within a few dozen yards of an enormous cone-shaped UFO.

A trained stunt flyer, Westendorf had taken off from the Pelotas airport near the southern tip of Brazil when he spotted an enormous object just ahead. His radio call to the Pelotas tower at 10:30 confirmed it was no hallucination; though the tower did not have a radar device, they could see the object and requested a close range report.

As the Piper Apache approached, Westendorf, who did not believe in UFOs, realized it was unlike anything he had ever seen in his twenty years of flying. Over a period of fifteen minutes he managed to circle the huge brown object, which was spinning, three times, once bringing his tiny plane within 130 feet of it. Westendorf described it as a faceted cone with a round point on top and a wide flat bottom. Each of the object's eight to ten facets, or sloping side panels, featured three large, somewhat triangular bulges. He estimated the object to be about 225 feet high by 325 feet in diameter at its widest point.

After his third lap, Westendorf noticed a hole where the rounded top on the large object had been just moments before. Then, from out of this hole, rose a classic, saucer-shaped object, about thirty feet in diameter. Its long axis emerged vertically, cleared the larger object, then tipped down to a flat orientation and flew away at tremendous speed—about Mach 10, according to Westendorf.

Fearless, the pilot decided to fly over the top of the "mother ship," but abandoned the idea when it began to rotate more rapidly and fire red light beams from its top. When the craft shot straight up at tremendous speed, Westendorf at first thought the resulting shock wave might knock him out of the sky, but he never felt any turbulence. The entire incident was witnessed by three ground-based air traffic controllers and numerous other people on the beach at Pelotas, but the government's air defense system radar center at Curitiba never picked up the mystery object on their radar screens.

SOURCE: *Michael Lindemann*, CNI News, *Vol. 3 No. 20, December 20, 1997.*

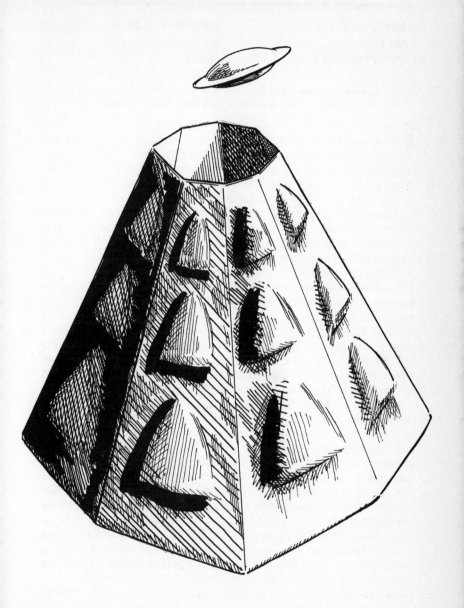

TYPE: *Triangular*	**DESCRIPTIVE INCIDENT**
VARIANT: *Diamond*	**DATE:** *December 29, 1980*
SKEPTIC'S SOLUTION: *Secret U.S. craft*	**LOCATION:** *Huffman, Texas*
	WITNESSES: *Betty Cash, Vickie and Colby Landrum*

The three witnesses were driving home to Dayton after dinner at a truck stop in New Caney when they saw a light above the trees. They didn't think much of it at first, but after rounding a curve onto a straight stretch of a desolate, two-lane highway, the light, now at less than treetop level, began to approach them.

Vickie Landrum, fearful of being burned alive, screamed for Betty Cash to stop the car. Cash thought they were seeing the Second Coming of Christ. She and Landrum then got out of the car to get a better look at the object, which was less than 130 feet away, but seven-year-old Colby's screams brought his aunt back into the car.

Cash walked to the front of the car to get a better look at the huge, upright, diamond-shaped object. The top and bottom of the intensely bright, metallic-colored "diamond" were cut off and flat rather than pointed. At the center of the diamond was a ring of small blue lights; occasionally, a cone-shaped flame shot out from its bottom. The heat it produced was such that the women could feel their faces burning. When Vickie Landrum grasped the dashboard, her fingers sunk into it, and when Cash tried to get back into the car, the door handle was so hot that she had to use her coat to open it.

Suddenly, with a blast of fire, the object rose into the sky. But just as it cleared the treetops, the witnesses saw helicopters swarm in from all directions. Cash restarted the car and five minutes later reached an intersection, where she pulled over and counted twenty-three helicopters flying around the object. Many of them were later identified as large, double-rotor, Boeing CH-47 Chinooks, but a 1982 investigation by the Department of the Army failed to ever locate just whose helicopters they were.

By the time Cash got home, she felt terribly sick. Her skin reddened, her eyes swelled, and the large knots that formed on her neck and scalp became blisters. She had a headache, felt nauseous, and thought she was about to die. The Landrums also looked sunburned and their stomachs were upset, but they were never as sick as Cash, who would be hospitalized more than twenty-five times in the years that followed, including two operations for cancer, even though she had never shown prior signs of it.

The helicopters, which were also seen by a policeman and his wife in the Huffman area that night, suggested to some investigators that the mystery object might have been a secret U.S. craft that had gotten out of control. But efforts by Cash and Landrum to get answers from government agencies went nowhere, and a lawsuit seeking compensation from the U.S. government for their injuries was dismissed by U.S. District Court in 1986.

SOURCE: *John Schuessler*, The Cash-Landrum UFO Incident *(LaPorte, TX: Geo Graphics Printing, 1998).*

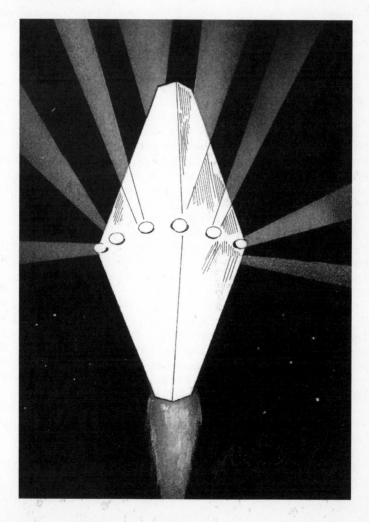

TYPE: *Triangular*	**DESCRIPTIVE INCIDENT**
VARIANT: *"Ice cream cone"*	**DATE:** *April 16, 1966*
SKEPTIC'S SOLUTION: *Satellite and Venus*	**LOCATION:** *Portage County, Ohio*
	WITNESSES: *Dale F. Spaur, Wilbur Neff, Wayne Huston, Frank Panzanella*

This one was made for Hollywood. Deputy Sheriff Dale Spaur and his deputy, Wilbur Neff, had been dispatched to answer a call about a car that had sheared a utility pole. While they were talking to an Ohio Edison repairman at 4:45 in the morning, a call came in over the police radio about a woman west of Portage County who had seen a brightly lit object "as big as a house" fly over her neighborhood. After exchanging jokes about this report with the repairman, Dale and Neff headed west on Route 224 then turned around and stopped to investigate a car parked on the shoulder of the road. At one point Spaur looked around and saw "this thing" rising up from the woods nearby. "It was so low that you couldn't see it until it was right on top of you," Spaur said. The bright object illuminated the area to such a degree that the policemen looked down at their hands and clothes to see if they were on fire. The only sound they heard was a hum.

Terrified, Dale and Neff quickly sought the safety of their car. The object hovered over them for some time before it began moving east. Spaur finally picked up the police radio and told the dispatcher: "This bright object is right over here . . ." Immediately the reply came back: "Shoot it." And thus began a seventy-mile chase and speeds as high as 105 miles per hour.

Forty miles east of where the chase began, police officer Wayne Huston was sitting in his police cruiser, spoke to Spaur on the radio, and joined the chase himself. Huston first saw the object while Spaur was about five miles away. Huston was standing beside his police cruiser when it passed right over him about eight hundred or nine hundred feet over Route 14. "It was shaped like an ice cream cone with a sort of partly melted-down top," Huston said. The point of the cone pointed down and the top resembled a dome. When Spaur and Neff came down the road after it, Huston fell in behind them. As the chase crossed the border into Pennsylvania, the officers tried to locate a police car on their heading.

At 5:20 in the morning Frank Panzanella, a police officer in Conway, Pennsylvania, was heading down Second Avenue when he saw a shining object to his right. He got out of the car and was looking at the object when Spaur and Huston pulled up. Panzanella had been watching the object, which he described as bright, 25 to 35 feet in diameter, and shaped like "half a football," for ten minutes or so. The object, which was about one thousand feet in the air, then began moving, stopped suddenly, and finally "went straight up real fast to about 3,500 feet," according to Panzanella. The officers watched as the object rose until it was as small as a "ballpoint pen," passed to the left of the moon, then continued to "shoot straight up and disappear."

Major Hector Quintanilla, then head of the Air Force's Project Blue Book, believed that the four police officers in three independent police cars had first seen a satellite (though none was visible at that time over Ohio, according to Blue Book's consultant in astronomy, J. Allen Hynek) and had transferred their attention to Venus (which was seen by the observers when the object was also in sight). "A more lucid example of the disregard of evidence unfavorable to a preconceived explanation could hardly be found," Hynek concluded.

SOURCE: *J. Allen Hynek*, The UFO Experience: A Scientific Inquiry, *(Chicago: Henry Regnery, 1972).*

TYPE: *Triangular*	**DESCRIPTIVE INCIDENT**
VARIANT: *"Top"*	DATE: *July 1, 1977*
SKEPTIC'S SOLUTION: *Moon or*	LOCATION: *Aviano, Italy*
"earthquake lights"	WITNESSES: *Sergeant Roger Furry,*
	Benito Manfré, and many others

NATO's Aviano Air Base in Italy is operated by the U.S. Air Force under the control of the Italian Defense Ministry. At three o'clock on a clear, warm summer morning, with the moon still fairly high in the sky, at least eighteen personnel on the base observed a strange object buzzing like a swarm of bees just beyond the perimeter fence.

The event began with a call from the security policeman in the control tower located at the corner of the Victor Alert facility, where aircraft stand ready for immediate launch in the event of hostilities. He reported that all the alarms on the fence's motion and magnetic detectors had gone off at the same time. The guard immediately noticed an unusual light just off base to the northwest. At the same time the facility experienced a power outage and, although the auxiliary power system kicked in immediately, minor power fluxes continued for another fifteen minutes or so. When the guard contacted the nearby Security Police Control Center, Sergeant Roger Furry notified the Wing Command Post and informed them that a security response team had been dispatched to the area.

A few minutes later Furry went outdoors to see the very bright object himself. The multiple lights around the rim of the object made it difficult for Furry to discern its shape, but other witnesses would describe it as looking like a spinning top. The lights on the object, which he estimated to be some seventy-five to one hundred feet in diameter, changed from yellow, to orange, to red. Furry said the object hovered about thirty feet off the ground some fifteen hundred feet away on the other side of the fence. He watched the buzzing object for about five minutes before it headed toward the nearby Dolomite Mountains and, within a minute, disappeared.

Benito Manfré, a night watchman living near the base, also saw the "mass" of lights in the sky and noticed the power outage. The military claimed the object was merely the moon shining off some low clouds and later a geologist ventured that the object might actually have been an "earthquake light."

SOURCE: *Jerry Rolwes (Lt. Col. USAF Ret.), "The Mystery of Aviano,"* MUFON UFO Journal, *No. 334, February, 1996; "MUFON Forum: Update on Aviano,"* MUFON UFO Journal, *No. 367, November 1998; Timothy Good,* Above Top Secret, *(New York: Quill, 1988).*

TYPE: *Triangular*	**DESCRIPTIVE INCIDENT**
VARIANT: *Triangle*	**DATE:** *March 14, 1995*
SKEPTIC'S SOLUTION: *Helicopter or*	**LOCATION:** *St. Petersburg, Russia*
small aircraft	**WITNESSES:** *Mikhail Petrovich*
	Baryshok, Vasily Alexandrovich
	Istomin, many others

For many people in this venerable Russian city and its suburbs, this would be a day to remember. The first sightings were reported at 3:40 in the morning and described a bright orange star. Within a half hour another observer saw a bright glowing star "like a globe." But most of the sightings took place that evening beginning shortly after seven o'clock. People at various locations in and around the city began seeing a variety of objects, including a glowing yellow ellipse or flattened sphere, a yellow-orange disc with several large lights around its circumference, and "an upside down saucer divided into sections and rotating counterclockwise" with a "thin, triangular ray . . . coming from the center of the object and shining up perpendicularly."

But the best of the sightings came from personnel at the Pulkovo Airport air traffic control center. They began observing a strange object after being alerted to its presence by a woman driving in a car who asked, "What is going on?" So it was about 7:30 when Mikhail Petrovich Baryshok saw what looked like a distant triangular-shaped object to the north. From the vantage point of the tower balcony, he and others could see, through binoculars, that the eight separate lights stayed equidistant from one another on the object. "The object remained stationary until four or five smaller ones flew up to it," Baryshok recalled. All were white objects except the fifth, which was a reddish-white. These long, glowing bullet-like objects, he noted, did not seem entirely real.

The unknown object was tracked by their RLS radar, according to Vasily Alexandrovich Istomin, who was in charge of coordinating air traffic. "We saw a target over the city," he said. "It first moved from the northern part of St. Petersburg to the south, then it backtracked, then disappeared, reappeared, and disappeared once again." On the basis of the radar return, the slow moving object seemed to be about the size of a helicopter or small plane. According to Istomin, the military at Gorelovo Airport also tracked the object: "The military said that no aircraft should have been there."

The crew of an aircraft landing at Pulkovo Airport at that time also apparently saw the strange, glowing UFO. From the aircraft's altitude just above five thousand feet, the object appeared near the ground, over the houses. Istomin said the RLS tracked it at about eight hundred feet.

After watching the object, which "did not look like any traditional aircraft," for half a hour, Istomin said, "the UFO split into smaller objects that could not be seen visually or on radar." He did report seeing a transponder number for the object, but speculated that the object was using the code to pass unnoticed, or that "the computer recorded the nearest aircraft number."

SOURCE: *Michael S. Boruch, "Close Encounters over St. Petersburg, March 14, 1995,"* International UFO Reporter, *Winter 1995.*

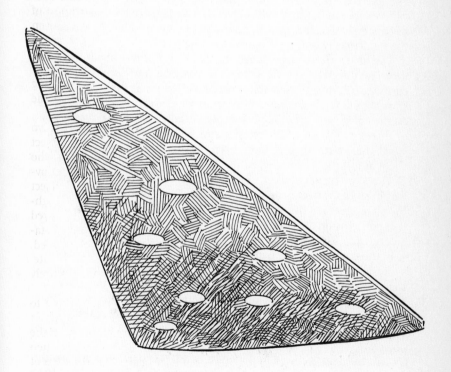

TYPE: *Triangular*
VARIANT: *"Boomerang"*
SKEPTIC'S SOLUTION: *"Stunt" pilots*

DESCRIPTIVE INCIDENT
DATE: *July 24, 1984*
LOCATION: *Buchanan, New York*
WITNESSES: *"Carl," "Milton," and
others*

Eleven security guards at the Indian Point nuclear reactor complex on the Hudson River had witnessed a huge, brilliantly lit, boomerang-shaped object ten days previously, so on this night, when one of the guards said, "Hey, here comes that UFO again," five guards and two supervisors ran out to see the object. In the distance they saw lights in a semicircle, which turned from yellow to white to blue. In the rear of the semicircle was a single blinking red light.

The object slowly approached the plant until it was about five hundred feet directly above the witnesses. "Carl," a thirty-five-year-old security guard, thought the object was a solid mass as it blocked out the stars behind it. He described it as being the size of three football fields. As the object flew over the nuclear plant's only operational reactor (out of three) at the time, the entire alarm system failed. The guards just stood there with their mouths open, having been given the order to shoot at it if the object stopped.

The slow moving object, seen by plant workers as well as guards, was in sight for twenty minutes. One guard at a security console inside the plant observed the object via a security camera perched on a ninety-foot pole outside the building. He described seeing eight bright lights in a very wide V-shape, almost like a half circle. It was so large that to scan the entire object he had to pan the camera nearly 180 degrees.

Residents of nearby Peekskill saw the object at the same time, and the police department received numerous calls about the UFO that night. The UFO was also videotaped from Brewster, a town less than twenty miles away. An analysis of the tape by personnel at the Jet Propulsion Laboratory indicated that the lights were part of a *single* large object.

This incident occurred in the midst of a UFO "flap" that gripped the Hudson Valley region of New York, beginning on New Year's Eve 1982 and not letting up until about 1987. During this time the huge "Westchester boomerang," as it was known, was seen by thousands of people. But there is no doubt that at least some of the sightings were caused by a group of small planes flown by pilots from a small airport in Stormville, New York. The "stunt" pilots flew their planes in formation, sometimes cut their engines, and may have modified their navigation lights—in sum, making a mockery of flight safety regulations. But the FAA never managed to catch up with the phantom hoaxers.

SOURCE: *J. Allen Hynek and Philip J. Imbrogno with Bob Pratt,* Night Siege: The Hudson Valley UFO Sightings *(New York: Ballantine, 1987).*

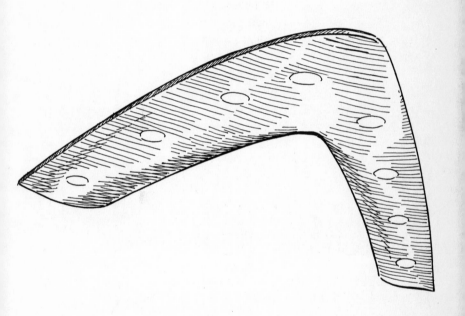

SHAPE-SHIFTER UFOs

TYPE: *Shape-shifter*	DESCRIPTIVE INCIDENT
VARIANT: *Flexible X*	DATE: *October 26, 1967*
SKEPTIC'S SOLUTION: *"Muscae volantes" (i.e., eyeball floaters)*	LOCATION: *Moinge Downs, Dorset, England*
	WITNESS: *Angus Brooks*

N umerous cross-shaped UFOs were seen over Britain during the fall of 1967. These very Christianlike "crosses" had a long vertical bar traversed by a shorter horizontal one. In the midst of this, a very responsible witness named Angus Brooks, who was a retired flight administrating officer of BOAC's Comet Flight, gave a remarkably detailed account of the flexing X-shaped object that some UFO researchers believed might have been responsible for the cross-shaped UFOs reported at the time.

At 11:25 on the morning of the incident, Brooks, dressed in a waterproof anorak and trousers, was walking his two dogs across the downs. The high winds led him to seek some shelter by lying down flat on his back in a shallow indentation on a hill. Shortly after watching a contrail disappear, a "craft" descended into view at "lightning speed." This craft consisted of a central circular chamber with one long, narrow fuselage at the front and three more narrow fuselages gathered together at the rear.

The craft then decelerated silently "with what appeared to be immensely powerful reverse thrust," Brooks noted, and leveled out 200 to 300 feet above the ground. As it slowed to a hover about a quarter mile away, two of the three rear fuselages opened up so that all four fuselages were now equidistant from one another. The craft then rotated ninety degrees and remained motionless for the next twenty-two minutes, unaffected by the strong winds.

The craft, Brooks said, seemed to be made of translucent material, taking on the color of the sky above it and changing as the clouds passed over it. The bottom of each fuselage was "ribbed," while each tip had an upward slant rather than the typical downward slant of the nose section of traditional aircraft. At 11:47 the two flexible fuselages closed up next to the fuselage that initially led the way, and the craft climbed at "light" speed, its trailing fuselage now in the lead.

Some tried to explain the Brooks sighting as "muscae volantes," or eyeball floaters.

SOURCE: *Angus Brooks, "Remarkable Sighting Near Dorset Coast,"* Flying Saucer Review, *14(1): 3–4, Jan./Feb. 1968.*

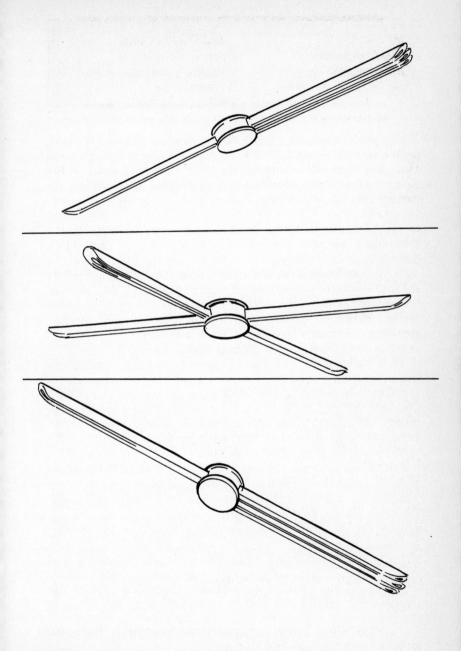

TYPE: *Shape-shifter*	**DESCRIPTIVE INCIDENT**
VARIANT: *Merging discs*	**DATE:** *November 2, 1968*
SKEPTIC'S SOLUTION: *Hoax*	**LOCATION:** *Southeastern France*
	WITNESS: *"Dr. X"*

The witness to one of the strangest UFO sightings on record is known only as Dr. X. A decade prior to his experience, he had stepped on a land mine in Algeria, leaving his right side partially paralyzed. A few days before the UFO incident he had been injured again, accidentally cutting a leg while chopping wood at his home in the southeast of France.

At approximately 3:55 A.M. on this November day, he was awakened by his infant son. After comforting him, Dr. X went to the kitchen for a glass of water then stepped out on the terrace. Approaching from the right were two luminous objects, moving down the valley in front of the house. The objects, shaped like one contact lens placed atop another, appeared to be clones: the top half of each glowed a silvery white, while the bottom halves were sunset-red in color. Both had three antennas, two small ones at either point or extremity, and a larger one on the top, as tall as the object was thick, pointing straight up.

From the bottom of each object a narrow beam or ray of white light was aimed at the ground. More light emanated from around the antennas, filling the narrowing distance between the two objects. Dr. X felt they were "sucking in the atmospheric electricity and that I could see it entering through the antennas and then exploding between the two objects, the whole thing producing one single glow of light."

The two glowing apparitions continued to draw closer to each other and then magically *merged* into a single object. The unified UFO, whose diameter would later be estimated at two hundred feet minus the antennas, then approached the terrace where Dr. X stood mesmerized. The object began a slow ninety-degree rotation, so that its bottom, still emitting the thin beam of light, was now perpendicular to the valley and facing the witness.

Just as Dr. X was struck by the beam of light, he heard a loud "bang," and the object itself evaporated into a whitish cloud that rapidly dissipated with the wind. A thin thread of light then rose high into the sky before vanishing as a white dot and exploding like Fourth of July fireworks.

The aftereffects would be as bizarre as the incident itself. The earlier self-inflicted ax cut was now virtually healed, followed over the next few days by a dramatic improvement in his old war wound. A week later, after a bout of stomach cramps, a reddish rash in the shape of an isosceles triangle appeared on Dr. X's abdomen. Soon his son would display the same symptoms simultaneously; these would come and go at roughly three week intervals for the next two years. Poltergeistlike phenomena also plagued the Dr. X household.

SOURCE: *Frank B. Salisbury*, The Utah UFO Display: A Biologist's Report *(Old Greenwich, CT: Devin-Adair, 1974), pp. 212–219.*

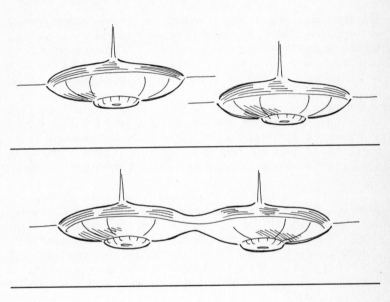

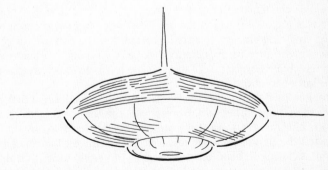

TYPE: *Shape-shifter*
VARIANT: *Morphing object*
SKEPTIC'S SOLUTION: *Unusual natural phenomenon*

DESCRIPTIVE INCIDENT
DATE: *June 29, 1954*
LOCATION: *Seven Islands, Quebec, Canada*
WITNESSES: *James Howard, Lee Boyd, H. McDonnell, and thirty passengers*

Shortly after taking off from New York, the British Overseas Airways Corporation (BOAC) Stratocruiser bound for London was put on a holding pattern over the coast of Rhode Island. After this unusual delay, Boston Air Traffic Control asked the pilot, Captain James Howard, to detour around Cape Cod on his way to a scheduled refueling stop at Goose Bay, Labrador.

Sometime later, as the plane was flying over the St. Lawrence River and Seven Islands, Quebec, Howard and his co-pilot, Lee Boyd, spotted a number of objects flying in and out of the broken cloud cover. The objects were below and three or four miles northwest of the BOAC flight, which was cruising along at an altitude of 19,000 feet with northeast heading.

As the plane crossed over into Labrador, the objects climbed well above the cloud layer and came into clear view of the BOAC crew and thirty passengers. Off the port side Howard saw seven objects—six small, oval-shaped objects strung out in a line ahead, and behind them, a much larger object. These shifted position, and sometimes the small objects were two ahead and four behind the large object, or sometimes three ahead and three behind, and so on. All the objects appeared solid and gray-colored.

Though the encounter lasted twenty minutes, the large object's shape was impossible to pin down. "The large object was continually, slowly, changing shape," reported Howard, "in the way that a swarm of bees might alter its appearance." A pear, a triangle, a boomerang, and a telephone handset were some of the forms Howard sketched out on his knee pad at the time.

Co-pilot Boyd then called the Goose Bay tower to tell them they were seeing something rather odd. In response, the tower vectored an F-94 on patrol in the area toward the airliner. When the BOAC flight crew contacted the fighter pilot, he reported having the airliner in sight on radar and closing in head-on at a distance of twenty miles. But during this conversation, Howard noticed that the small objects had disappeared. McDonnell, the navigator, reported that the small objects had actually converged on and "entered" the large object. Then, as the fighter approached, the crew saw the large object dwindle in size until it completely disappeared.

A UFO investigator for the University of Colorado's Condon Committee admitted this sighting was an unusual one, but concluded that some "natural phenomenon, which is so rare that it apparently has never been reported before or since," was responsible.

SOURCE: *James Howard, "The BOAC Labrador Sighting of 1954," Flying Saucer Review, 27 (6): 2–3, June 1982; Daniel S. Gillmor, editor,* Scientific Study of Unidentified Flying Objects *(New York: Bantam, 1969).*

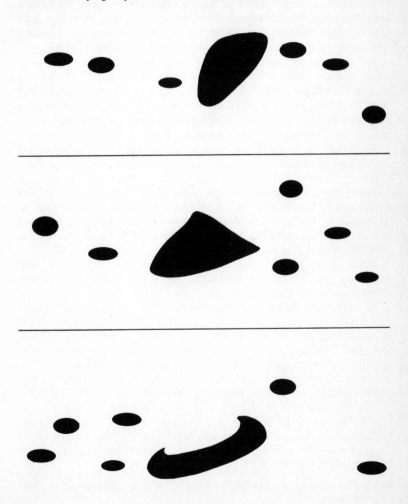

TYPE: *Shape-shifter*	**DESCRIPTIVE INCIDENT**
VARIANT: *"Glob"*	**DATE:** *1982*
SKEPTIC'S SOLUTION: *Hallucination*	**LOCATION:** *Central Valley, California*
	WITNESSES: *"Keith Boyer" and friend*

At two o'clock in the morning, "Keith Boyer" and a friend were driving north at seventy miles per hour on Interstate 5. They were about halfway to San Francisco from Los Angeles when they spotted a little flashing light floating just above the highway several miles ahead. There was little traffic on the road and no one was behind them.

As their car approached the light, the two men began discussing what the light could be. An airplane? A police patrol? A crop-dusting helicopter? But they rejected all their own explanations as inappropriate. "The object was a series of lights, seemingly merging and rotating into each other, with a kind of indefinable mist surrounding the object—a fuzzy atmospheric phenomenon," Boyer noted.

Then the object, which had been hovering about a hundred feet off the ground, began to descend, and the light itself became "uncomfortably bright"—a mix of deep rich blues, greens, yellows, and reds.

When Boyer's car pulled abreast of the object, it was not more than a hundred feet or so over to the side of the highway. But instead of feeling elated, Boyer, who had spent years studying UFOs, was horrified by the sight. "It seemed to me that the object wasn't a spaceship" but "something that was an entity into itself, or unto itself," he said.

Boyer found it hard to describe the object since its perspective kept shifting. It was about fifty feet across, roughly circular, "but oozing, changing, transmogrifying," he recalled.

At some point a beam of light from the UFO swung across the field and struck their car. After a blackout period, the next thing Boyer remembers was that he was no longer driving; his friend was. And the two were "babbling" to each other in some unknown tongue. After ten or fifteen minutes their strange mental state gradually wore off. The two men did not speak to each other about the incident for a long time; neither witness was willing to undergo hypnosis.

This sighting of a large, organic-looking glob supports the notion, once held seriously by such people as Kenneth Arnold, that UFOs could be living creatures whose home was outer space or the Earth's upper atmosphere. Trevor James Constable, the aviation historian, occultist, and contactee, called these aerial entities "critters."

SOURCE: **Preston E. Dennett**, One in Forty: The UFO Epidemic *(New York: Kroshka Books, 1997).*

AFTERWORD

SIZING UP SHAPES

From the reports collected here, we can see that UFOs range in size alone from small balls of light barely six inches in diameter to giant, flying wing- or triangle-shaped objects described in terms of football fields. Reports even exist of unidentified aerial objects as large as aircraft carriers.

Certain connections exist, however, between an object's size and shape. The larger the UFO, the more likely it is to be shaped like a cigar, flying wing, or triangle. Curiously (and everything about UFOs is curious in one form or another), "windows" or "portholes" are often associated with the cigars. The "classic" flying suacer—the circular, disc-shaped object almost everyone associates with UFOs—populates the vast mid-range of reported sizes, anywhere from a few feet to 200 to 300 feet across. The most commonly reported diameters fall in the 35- to 50-foot range. Egg- and perfectly sphere-shaped UFOs tend, again, generally speaking, to represent objects less than fifty feet across. Obviously, there is some overlap in all the categories, which can be attributed either to the phenomenon itself or to the vagaries of human perception and the inherent difficulties of accurately judging size and shape.

Size and shape also seem to correlate with behavior to some extent. Large cigar-shaped objects, for example, are frequently referred to in the literature as "mother ships," because they have been seen emitting smaller UFOs. For whatever reason, flying wings and triangles seem to be a solitary phenomenon, rarely accompanied by smaller UFOs. In the same vein, giant UFOs of whatever shape are rarely, if ever, involved in close encounter or landing cases, which makes for a certain technological sense: they would be more difficult to land, assuming a large enough space could even be found.

By contrast, the classic disc is quite often encountered both close up and on the ground. On such occasions, legs, poles, or columns, and other means of support are routinely reported. Small egg-shaped and elliptical UFOs also seem to be reported in closer proximity to the surface than the other categories, and, more often that not, with apparent legs attached. This, again, makes for common sense, both technologically and psychologically. If all such accounts were total fabrications, in other words, the purported "witnesses" would logically require some sort of support mechanism for the object of their fancy.

But logic and common sense may not be infallible tools when it comes to unlocking the UFO mystery. Given that the objects are routinely reported as capable of hovering in place like a mechanical hummingbird, why not suppose they could hover just as effortlessly inches off the ground as at an altitude of several hundred or thousand feet? By the same token, though, why would a witness (such as Father Gill, see page 52) "attach" support appendages to a UFO hovering in midair, where none were clearly needed? Still, the presence of reported, apparently retractable, supports makes for common sense, while seemingly supporting the physical (as opposed, say, to the atmospheric or psychological) nature of the phenomenon.

UFO FASHIONS

Another part of the puzzle is why a particular shape seems to enjoy a certain vogue for a brief period of time, only to be overshadowed months or years later by an entirely different one. Why should the classic saucer shape be "popular" in one year (or culture), cigar or rocket shapes in another, and giant, triangle shapes in yet a third? Perhaps the phenomenon itself simply changes form over time and place. After all, we've already seen that some UFOs can apparently change shape at will or whim, apart from the angle at which they're viewed. Perhaps UFOs "prefer" changes in general form over time, too, in the same way that human tastes in fashion come and go. Or, metaphorically speaking, maybe cigars are from Mars, saucers from Venus, and triangles from Pluto, or their extraterrestrial equivalents, although that seems highly unlikely.

Of course a skeptic would say that the mundane stimuli which give rise to UFO reports remain relatively static, and that it is the human observer who changes in response to cultural fads and fashions, which in turn are influenced and driven by media attention. Thus, time and place take precedent over the phenomenon, and indeed, in the case of UFOs, *generate* the phenomenon in the first place.

A prime example in the skeptical scrapbook would be cases of the "Great American Airship" seen between 1896 and 1897. Airship reports fell into two general categories, cigar- or dirigible-shaped, and those in which the Airship resembled a sort of mechanical bird, with giant, flapping (or rigid) wings. Both categories also involved reports of a human crew onboard, and bright searchlight beams when seen at night.

Not exactly your classic UFO in either event. Skeptics would attribute the reports to a sort of "psychic outbreak" or anticipation of heavier-than-air flight, an idea that was the subject of much popular speculation at the time, but that wouldn't be realized for another six years. One of the questions skeptics don't address is *where did the Airship mania go* between 1897 and its next eruption in Great Britain, some fifteen years later? For that matter, where were the mysterious Airship sightings in the immediate wake of the 1903 Wright brothers flight? Now that we really *could* fly, why no more phantom Airship reports in this country?

The British Airship reports that preceded the outbreak of the First World War are curious in the same regard. In the main, they consist not of sightings of noisy biplanes, increasingly in terrestrial vogue, but of large, cylindrical, Zeppelinlike objects, again bearing searchlight beams by night. It is not until the 1930s, in the cases of the Scandinavian "ghost flier," that ordinary airplanes masquerade as modern day UFOs via near impossible circumstances and behavior.

These early aerial object "scares" remain a source of much discussion and controversy, and it's worth noting that not all ufologists heartily embrace them. More fashionable among ufologists are the foo fighters and ghost rockets that immediately preceded the flying saucer outbreak in the summer of 1947. All three occurred in relatively rapid succession; taken together, they cause problems for the skeptical notion of media influence and/ or generation because they differ so radically from one another. To simplify, if everyone were reading the same newspaper, they should be predisposed, more or less, to see and report the same thing. But this was patently not the case. Foo fighters, seen during the closing days of the Second World War in both the European and Pacific Theaters, were invariably described as nocturnal balls of colored light, and so reported in the *New York Times* and other papers. But the so-called Scandinavian ghost rockets of 1946, also reported in this country, were a daytime affair characterized by cigar or torpedo shapes. By the following summer, in the wake of the Arnold sighting, UFOs had taken a decidedly circular turn, appearing predominantly as the classic daylight disc, or popular flying saucer.

Why the abrupt change? If media reports had somehow primed the populace to "see" novel aerial objects in a certain light, then why doesn't the 1947 wave begin with nocturnal lights or daylight rockets, both of which preceded it in the press? We are not arguing, however, that foo fighters and ghost rockets were either progenitors or reflections of some pervasive UFO phenomenon. Our stance is much simpler: sometimes people see something odd and unusual, and report it to the best of their ability.

J. Allen Hynek once wondered why, despite the many various objects reported, even more wondrous ones weren't—especially if UFOs were predominantly the product of a hyperactive, almost infinite, human imagination. Where were the reports of flying pink elephants, he wondered rhetorically, a mythical figure popularly associated with a hallucinatory drinking binge? And then, from France, came a report of just such a creature. Passengers on one side of a French airplane reported seeing a pink elephant rising through the clouds in the distance. Upon investigation, it turned out that a large circus balloon—in the form of a pink elephant—had broken loose from its moorings below.

As a fashion statement, however, pink elephants were a veritable bust on the UFO runway, putting on only this onetime show. But certain other trends were evident. The 1947 sightings, characterized but not limited to daylight disc reports, were followed by a major outbreak of sightings in 1952, which were dominated by reports of nocturnal lights. France played host to an outbreak the year after, and here the largely oval or elliptical UFOs often appeared on the ground and in association with little beings, again a sharp departure from every UFO that had come before. France would also give birth to reports of vertical-standing, cigar-shaped UFOs during roughly the same period.

More recently, in the mid-1980s, the Hudson Valley area of New York was haunted by reports of huge flying-wing or boomerang-shaped UFOs reportedly as wide as several football fields. Around the same time, Brazilians were reporting relatively small, refrigerator-shaped UFOs which gave off burning beams of light. At the end of the decade, giant, triangular UFOs, or at least reports of them, would invade Belgium. Today, these dark-colored, triangular-shaped UFOs seem almost omnipresent, threatening to overtake the classic saucer as the world's most popular UFO shape.

The growing number of alleged alien abductions in recent years only exacerbates the UFO "fashion" problem. In many if not most instances, *no UFO is seen from an outside perspective at all,* at least not in the traditional sense. All too often abductees merely report a bedroom encounter with small entities which reportedly whisk them away, either physically or in a beam of light. They then typically report finding themselves inside an evenly lighted room, where they are physically examined and which they *assume* to be within a classic flying saucer, whatever that is.

We admit to being baffled as well. It would be the height of hubris to suggest that the UFO phenomenon manifests in a complete cultural vacuum, far from the madding crowd of media and other social influences. But the opposite viewpoint is equally absurd. Reporters theoretically tired of one kind of UFO don't routinely knock on doors in hopes of finding another one—or they would get nothing else done. In the main, it's the wit-ness(es) who rings *them*. Instead of leading the UFO parade, the media merely bring up the rear.

The parade itself deserves our attention. Is the UFO phenome-non capable of mercurially changing clothes in the same way that we casually switch between a T-shirt and tuxedo? Or is the UFO only a naked, fairy tale Emperor, bereft of all clothing, save for those royal robes and gorgeous, glittering garments we collec-tively project?

PHYSICAL EVIDENCE

Aside from anecdotal accounts, UFO evidence also comes in pri-mary and secondary form. Primary evidence might be considered detection by instrumentation, such as by radar or photographic equipment. We've known since at least the summer of 1952, fol-lowing a series of radar/visual sightings over Washington Na-tional Airport, that UFOs sometimes show up on radar. More often than not, though, they *don't* seem to register on radar. We also know that radar itself is subject to false readings from a variety of factors, including internal malfunctions and external atmospheric conditions, such as temperature inversions. A bent radar beam can even "lock" onto a moving object on the ground or the surface of the water, which subsequently appears to be airborne to the radar system.

Literally thousands of claimed UFO photographs now exist, from still snapshots to, increasingly, extended videos taken by handheld camcorders. Yet not a single photo or set of photos can be pinpointed as absolutely and unambiguously conclusive, although several remain highly suggestive after analysis. Some-what ironically, ufologists as a whole tend to "prefer" slightly flawed pictures to the perfect ones, such as the hundreds of stills and film submitted by Edward Meier of Switzerland, under the assumption that if something sounds or looks too good to be true, it probably isn't. Some ufologists reject many of Ed Walter's Gulf Breeze pictures on the same grounds, while others argue that there's just enough ambiguity in his photos to render them believable.

Computerized analysis is hardly conclusive when it comes to the photographic evidence. While camera technology has increased exponentially in sophistication, so, alas, has the computer software that allows for image manipulation. Hoaxers, it would appear, keep pace with the times, just like the rest of us.

Secondary evidence exists in the form of physical traces—alleged impacts left on the environment (and sometimes on the human observer, see page 112) by the presence or passage of a UFO. UFO researcher Ted Phillips has catalogued more than 4,000 physical trace cases to date. These traces run a veritable gauntlet of physical effects, from dehydrated or singed ground and grass, to broken tree limbs, circular "scars" on pavement and in annual crops, to odd burns and other "radiation"-like effects reported by human eyewitnesses.

At Delphos, Kansas, in November 1971, a mushroom-shaped UFO reportedly left behind a glowing ring on the ground. When the ring area was sampled later, the soil was found remarkably resistant to water absorption compared to nearby control samples. In other instances, reported physical effects left behind in the UFO's wake include mutilated animals, so-called crop circles, and, of course, abducted humans, with their accounts of small, "scoop-mark" scars, nosebleeds, and implants.

Unfortunately, very little of the claimed physical evidence addresses the issue of UFO shape and size, and these cases will always be haunted by the specter of human hoaxing. As anyone who has closely followed the history of the crop circle phenomenon is forced to admit, the evidence is now almost overwhelming that they are the product of human hoaxers, or "landscape artists," as some prefer to be called. Certainly, any pretext of an argument that they represent an impression left by a landed UFO has long since evaporated in the presence of their increasingly complex and outrageous outlines. No UFO in recorded history that we are aware of in any way resembles a fractal, Mandlebrot set, or any other of the fantastic shapes that now routinely appear every summer in southern England and other areas around the world. Nor it is likely that these aftereffects are an artifact of the UFO's propulsion system rather than its shape.

The pre-crop-circle-craze UFO traces are more convincing. Among the best of these was a case that took place in Langenburg, Saskatchewan, Canada, in September 1974. Five spinning, dome-shaped UFOs were seen rising from the ground in broad daylight. The swirled traces left behind, which matched the witness's description in terms of diameter of the original objects, were discovered immediately in the wake of their departure and subsequently investigated and photographed by the Royal Canadian Mounted Police. A somewhat similar case had occurred at Tully, Queensland, Australia, in January 1966, which gave birth to the phrase "saucer nest" to describe such aftereffects.

Another subset of physical trace cases refers to ground marks reportedly left by legs or other support mechanisms lowered by the UFO upon landing. Typically, such traces represent simple holes or impressions left at intervals on the ground at least roughly corresponding to the witness's account of the object.

Socorro is a classic case in question (see p. 72). It is possible to deduce some information about the craft that landed at Socorro from the set of depressions found in the desert ravine immediately after the incident took place on April 24, 1964. The object apparently left behind four "landing pad" marks in an asymmetric arrangement. Three of the four marks were a couple of inches deep with a small mound of dirt pushed up and away from the center of each equilateral pad mark; the fourth mark was only one inch deep and ill-defined. It has been estimated that you would need the gentle settling of something weighing at least a ton to produce each pad mark left in that type of desert soil. The vehicle itself, then, must have weighed several tons. (A pancake-shaped craft that left marks on railroad ties during a landing in Quarouble, France, on September 10, 1954, was calculated to weigh about thirty tons.)

While the apparent weight of the Socorro object is impressive on its own, even more impressive is the layout of the object's "landing marks." No hoaxer in his or her right mind would ever have left the peculiar asymmetrical landing marks found at Socorro. The marks suggest a quadrilateral figure with the distance between the pad marks ranging from 9 feet 7½ inches, to 13 feet

2½ inches. But significantly, when lines are drawn from opposite pad marks, they cross in the center at ninety-degree angles. A careful engineering analysis by William T. Powers in 1968 showed that the various unequal measurements were internally consistent. Powers noted that if the center of gravity of the object was directly over the central burn mark that was also found on the ground, then equal weight would be supported at each mid-point of the lines drawn between the four landing pads—assuming the linkage among the "legs" was flexible.

"We must conclude," wrote Powers in the British journal *Flying Saucer Review*, "that everything argues in favour of the hypothesis that a vehicle landed near Socorro, on four pads." Powers was surprised to find that the landing pads seemed to have been placed "to serve the convenience of those using the vehicle (the footprints, and presumably the door, were located next to the mark that appears most 'misplaced') rather than according to a compulsive attachment to symmetry . . . And they do so," Powers noted with considerable astonishment, "without sacrificing any requirements for good engineering."

INSIDE SCOOP

If UFOs are indeed real physical objects, they are either solid all the way through like a coin, or they contain a compartment of some sort on the inside to house its "pilots" or "occupants." There are accounts of the insides of UFOs, and these come from two seemingly very disparate groups of "witnesses": contactees and abductees. Contactees came into prominence in the early 1950s with a series of books by George Adamski, Orfeo Angelucci, Truman Bethurum, Howard Menger, and others, in which they claimed to have made peaceful contact with the UFOs and their occupants. Not surprisingly, given that the early contactees were predominantly male, not a few of the ufonauts turned out to be females from known planets in the solar system. (Venus was especially popular.) But all ufonauts—male and female—were resolutely wise and benign; to an alien, they had come to warn us that we were polluting and otherwise endangering our home planet, primarily by continuing to manufacture atomic bombs.

Most aliens reported by contactees were borderline or super-Aryan types in appearance, but not all. In his 1954 book, *Aboard a Flying Saucer*, Truman Bethurum described his main contact, Aura Rhanes, as "tops in looks," a "gorgeous woman, shorter than any of the men, neatly attired, and also having a Latin appearance: coal black hair and olive complexion." Contactees tended to describe UFO interiors in the same, vague stereotypical terms. Finding himself inside a "huge, misty soap bubble," Orfeo Angelucci described its insides as stunningly beautiful, "made of an ethereal mother-of-pearl stuff, iridescent with exquisite colors that gave off light."

Contactee Daniel Fry, in *The Incident at White Sands*, claimed to have been allowed inside a remote-controlled "cargo carrier" that had settled on the desert floor outside Las Cruces, New Mexico, on the night of July 4, 1950. He described it as a silent "ovate spheroid about thirty feet in diameter . . . [and] about sixteen feet" thick, polished silver in color. An aperture opened, and Fry entered into a small enclosure, nine by seven and six feet high, with curved walls beveled at top and bottom. In the center of the floor of this small cell were four contour chairs arranged in pairs. On the rear wall was a sort of lens that projected a diffuse light. Fry said he was flown over several major American cities and then returned to the White Sands Proving Ground.

Conveniently, most of the flying saucers on which contactees were inevitably given a guided tour of the solar system also contained ordinary windows or portholes—presumably the better to glimpse the far side of the moon and the surface of Venus. But on the whole, mainstream ufology wasn't impressed with these contactee accounts. The largest organization of the time, the National Investigations Committee on Aerial Phenomena (NICAP), downplayed any UFO report involving humanoids, but especially contactee claims, which were dismissed as incredulous on their surface.

Abductees, however, are another story altogether. Instead of meeting advanced humans from another planet and then engaging them in protracted philosophical discussions, abductees often report frightening encounters with alien entities who physically remove them to a waiting UFO. While contactees sometimes met their contacts in restaurants, barber shops, and other public places in broad daylight, abductees report isolated, nocturnal encounters, usually on a deserted stretch of country road or other remote area, or, increasingly, in their own bedrooms.

In September 1961, a New Hampshire couple, Betty and Barney Hill, reported being taken inside a UFO that had stopped their car late at night, as they were returning from a vacation in Canada (see page 48). The Hills described a much "busier," apparently more realistic interior than their contactee predecessors; for one thing, the internal compartments and corridors seemed to coincide with the UFO's circular external shape. Betty was first seated on a stool underneath a bright light, before being laid upon a horizontal table, where she was subjected to an even more detailed physical examination, during which various exotic instruments were employed. As with contactee accounts, however, Betty engaged her captors in prolonged dialogue. She asked for proof of the experience and was handed a book by the alien in charge (a gift that was later retracted). At another point she said she would like to know where they come from, and the "leader" pulled down a wall map portraying a series of stars, some with interconnecting lines that were subsequently interpreted as "trade routes." With their memories partially erased, the Hills were then released and completed their drive home.

Subsequent abductees would report guided tours of the UFO's innards. Indeed, in *Abductions: The Measure of a Mystery*, University of Indiana folklorist Eddie Bullard identified the interior tour as one of several discrete episodes earmarking the "average" abduction. In temporal order, the stages are capture, examination, conference, tour, otherworldly journey, epiphany, and, ultimately, release, or return. Bullard sandwiched these seven stages between an eighth bookend event, which he referred to as "doorway amnesia." For some reason, abductees were better able to recall the time spent inside the UFO than they were those moments when they first entered or exited the object.

Nebraska police sergeant Herbert Schirmer's account is "typical" in this regard. In the early morning hours of December 3, 1967, he encountered a disc-shaped UFO that disgorged several short entities. Schirmer entered the ship via a ladder and found himself in a room 26 feet long and 20 feet wide. Red light came from strips set in the ceiling. Above a control panel and two triangle-back chairs was what he called a "vision screen." One of the beings explained that this was an "observation craft with a crew of four men" from a mother ship, or "interplanetary station," positioned in deep space. Schirmer said he was shown "things that look like computer machines," which he felt were putting things in his mind. In another area he was shown the vision screen's remote control device, described as a ball six feet in diameter, from which light and sound were transmitted. The ship's power system, which "operated through reversible electromagnetism," was a "crystallike rotor in the center . . . linked to two large columns."

In more recent abductee accounts, the ship's package tour seems to have been superceded by a single destination. David Jacobs, a Temple University historian and author of several UFO abduction studies, says that because abductees are brought on board the craft for one reason—the production of human-alien hybrids—they are privy to a limited portion of the UFO's interior. Some remember being ushered through a curved metallic corridor before arriving at the center of the vessel, which serves as the "medical area." These surroundings are clean, Spartan and clinical in appearance. There is medical apparatus everywhere—in drawers and on carts, and on the walls and ceilings. They describe the examination table as being "hard" and having lighted armlike devices attached to its sides. The room itself has a domed ceiling, windows like skylights, and gray or white walls.

There are also reports of "visiting rooms" involving benches and nurserylike enclosures where the abductees are shown and sometimes encouraged to nurse or handle what appear to be hybrid babies. Only rarely do abductees get to pass through what looks like a control room, which some describe as consisting of a windowless room, a console with lights, and seats that look unpadded.

One other curiosity about UFO interiors should also be mentioned, implausible as it sounds. People who claim to have seen the insides of these things sometimes report that the interiors are much larger than external appearance would otherwise indicate. This larger-inside-than-out-feeling featured prominently in a case from the early 1960s. One evening, a forty-nine-year-old man, known only as "Michel," had approached an enormous object sitting on the ground of a farm near Bray-sur-Seine in France. Sticking out from the bottom of the disc-shaped object was a column, about four feet wide, with a large vertical opening. Looking inside this illuminated opening, Michel saw an immense space nearly four times the diameter of the column itself. This huge cylindrical room, which was filled with apparatus displaying moving lights, had no apparent ceiling.

As strange as it sounds, this bigger-on-the-inside-than-out impression is exactly what a three dimensional creature like Michel or any one of us might expect to experience when confronted with a four dimensional space. An analysis of the geometry by Stan Kulikowski in the *MUFON UFO Journal* concluded: "Whether this inside-too-big phenomenon is actual alien technology or deliberate fraud or a subconscious psychological trick of perception, it is nevertheless based on good mathematics and related to the fundamental physics of our universe."

In sum, while the abductee accounts of UFO interiors represent something of an "improvement" over those of their contactee counterparts, when all is said and done, a somewhat similar taste remains in the mouth. For all their detail, they still don't strike the modern ear as *detailed enough*. With the sole exception of contactee/abductee Whitley Streiber, who once described dirty clothes piled in one corner of the chamber in which he found himself, UFO interiors seem a bit too antiseptic and unlived in. We don't expect wads of chewing gum stuck to the bottom of the examination table, but there is a pronounced absence of what might be described as both the accoutrements and castoffs of everyday life—the dripping faucet, the coffee cup on the counter, the lightbulb on the blink, the overflowing wastebasket in one corner of the room—or their alien equivalents, anyway.

But perhaps future technology will have banished these daily annoyances to the scrap heap of history, just as we have the slide rule and cloth diaper. Or maybe the aliens are just unearthly neat.

EXTRAORDINARY MANEUVERS

One reason why UFOs are referred to as *Unidentified* Flying Objects is because they behave and/or maneuver in ways not normally associated with identifiable mundane objects such as airplanes, helicopters, and balloons, or, for that matter, stars and planets.

Aside from their initial odd appearance, many witnesses say their attention was drawn by an object's unusually high rate of speed. We've seen this was the case with Kenneth Arnold, who estimated a speed of 1,750 mph for the nine silvery objects he saw near Mount Rainier, Washington, in 1947. Since then, speeds easily ten times that and more have been reported of UFOs. Unfortunately, such estimates are subject to the perils of perception—particularly as to distance—and so it wouldn't be overly surprising for them to be off by several orders of magnitude. Also, terrestrial technology has "caught up" to UFO technology, so to speak, in the last half century. Today's high-performance jet aircraft fly much faster and higher than they did fifty, twenty-five, or even ten years ago.

But while the sheer speed of some UFOs can now be conceivably accounted for, some other commonly reported characteristics can't. To the best of our knowledge, for example, the greater the speed, the more the noise. And today's jet engines don't just make noise, they make a lot of noise, as anyone who lives near an airport or military air base can attest. The decibels increase astronomically when jet planes break the sound barrier (approximately 670 mph at sea level). The exception to the speed equals noise rule is the modern helicopter. Although technology has made tremendous strides in this area as well, the majority of civilian and military "choppers" are notoriously noisy, especially in close proximity. (Sound at a distance can be influenced by several factors, including direction of travel of the sound-emitting object, wind direction relevant to the object and observer, and so on.)

Yet UFOs are almost uniformly silent in operation, whether seen at a distance or close up. In those cases where an audible sound is heard and reported (and in a handful of cases recorded), it is usually described as either a steady, low-pitched him, like that of an electrical transformer, or a repetitive, high-pitched "beep," much like the radio signal given off by the Soviet Union's Sputnik, the world's first artificial satellite.

Apart from high sustained flight speeds, UFOs are also reported as capable of extremely high rates of acceleration and deceleration while in level flight, or while going to or from a relatively stationary position. Countless cases describe a hovering UFO that suddenly shoots straight up or off at an angle, vanishing from view in seconds. Silent hovering accompanied by almost instantaneous acceleration would seem to rule out any known helicopters as a mundane UFO stimulus, along with lighter-than-air blimps and propeller and jet-propelled aircraft.

Hovering UFOs, on occasion, have vanished from view so rapidly that witnesses use terms like "disappeared in place," or "winked out" to describe the experience. From his analysis of several "disappearing" UFOs caught on video, however, physicist Bruce Maccabee has suggested that *all* disappearing UFOs might instead be instances of immediate acceleration. The UFO simply accelerates away too rapidly for the human eye to track or register it.

Many witnesses report equally "impossible" trajectories while the UFO is in flight, the most mentally challenging being the execution of acute right-angle (ninety-degree) turns, an apparent violation of known physics that would consign any living thing inside the UFO to a rather grisly demise. This could arguably represent a perceptual error on the part of the witness, even exaggeration. But even if true ninety-degree turns are discounted on the grounds of physical impossibility, we still find many accounts in which the UFO is said to follow an abrupt, zigzag path as opposed to a straight line or gently curving trajectory.

Nor should zigzag descriptions be confused with satellite "wobble," a known optical illusion associated with distant objects. To experience the latter for yourself, simply step outdoors some night and wait for one of the many artificial satellites that now pass routinely overhead by the hour. Although the satellite is traveling in a perfectly straight line, it will appear to wobble back and forth slightly, as if tracing out an extremely shallow or flattened sine wave. What's really happening is that your eyes are moving ever so slightly back and forth in an attempt to maintain focus, giving the impression that it is the satellite itself wobbling in orbit. Stationary point sources of light, like stars and planets, can appear to jump and move about under the same circumstances.

The clue here to a TRUFO, or "true UFO" (Maccabee's phrase), versus an IFO, or Identified Flying Object, is mainly one of *duration*. If the "UFO" seems to jump about but remains in the same relative position hour after hour, the overwhelming odds are that it is an astronomical body. If it merely wobbles slowly and merrily on its way, chances are it's a satellite or space shuttle.

Finally, there is what is known as the "falling-leaf" syndrome. Typically, this maneuver is associated with a hovering UFO that then descends to or near ground level. It has also been referred to as the pendulum motion, a gentle rocking back and forth during descent. To emulate the effect, drop a coin into a fishbowl or aquarium and watch its repeating S-shaped motion as it drops through the liquid medium to the bottom of the bowl.

The slow motion pendulum effect and the rapid zigzag motion, while at opposite ends of the reported speed and trajectory spectrum, are equally perplexing in that both maneuvers seem totally superfluous, or gratuitous, for want of better words. After all, the shortest distance between two points in classical physics is a straight line. So why do at least *some* UFOs seem to beat about the bush, so to speak, in terms of trajectories? Is it because they *want* to attract attention to themselves?

We don't profess to know. Physics tell us, however, that objects tend to travel in straight lines unless influenced by factors like gravity or intelligent, powered direction. Both the zigzag and leaf motion, then, raise the issue of whether or not UFOs are intelligently controlled from within (or without, if one wants to postulate remote-controlled robotic drones). The other "impossible" maneuvers present a second set of problems no less perplexing or significant than the first. Even if we grant UFOs intelligent occupants, what is it they are in control of? How, in short, do these unidentified objects *fly?*

MODES OF PROPULSION

An underlying complaint of ufology has always been the failure of mainstream science to take the subject seriously. But science is conservative by nature; it doesn't take gladly to things that supposedly defy the laws of physics, as when a UFO hovers stationary in space and then suddenly shoots out of sight. To most physicists, acceleration from a standing stop simply doesn't "work" that way, at least not with normal propulsion systems, including jet engines and chemical rockets.

Another sticking point, especially for astronomers, is the vast distance that separates stars in interstellar space. At 186,000 miles per *second,* it takes light eight minutes to cross the 93 million miles separating the Earth and Sun. But travel times between solar systems, or stars, is measured in light *years.* When we look at our nearest neighbor in space, for example, Alpha Centuri, we see it not as it is now, but as it was 4.3 years ago, the time it takes for its light to reach us. To cover the same distance by a conventional chemical rocket, traveling at an as yet unattainable speed of 186,000 miles per hour, would require more than 15,000 years for a one-way trip. It would also require taking along a huge amount of mass (propellant) that would have to be converted into kinetic energy.

But conventional wisdom changes over time, as new discoveries and resulting technologies come into play. Our own space program now routinely employs a gravitational assist from nearby planets (or the Sun itself) to hurl payloads toward distant targets within our own solar system, picking up speed in the process. The gravitational field doesn't have to be "stored" aboard the ship, in other words, in order to take advantage of its energy. Think of the latter as an interest-free loan that never has to be repaid.

Could UFOs operate along similar principles, perhaps by directly manipulating gravity fields? Paul Hill seems to think they could. What makes his speculations worth considering is that for more than twenty-five years Hill was employed by the National Aeronautics and Space Administration (and its predecessor, the National Advisory Committee on Aeronautics) as an aeronautical engineer, and so knows whereof he speaks. But given Hill's situation—an intense interest in the subject due to a UFO sighting in the early 1950s while employed for an agency with a strict UFOs-are-of-no-importance policy—his detailed analysis of the situation would not see the light of day until after his death in 1990. Not surprisingly, the book, called *Unconventional Flying Objects: A Scientific Analysis,* has made Hill the darling of the pro-UFO intelligentsia.

Hill's book is not easily summarized. It begins with the obvious—UFOs have no visible means of propulsion—and ends in appendices for the mathematically adept. In between, he performs an analysis based on the data available, which is nowhere near as meager as the skeptics would have us believe. Hill focuses his engineering skills on such things as the most frequently observed characteristics of UFO flight—the tilt. UFOs often tilt forward to advance, tilt back to stop, bank to turn, etc. But a craft constrained by normal aerodynamics, like our own aircraft, would be incapable of making such motions. This tilting-to-perform-all-maneuvers turns out to be the ideal control method for a mode of propulsion that involves a repulsive force field, which somewhat resembles the sort of tension you feel when the like poles of two magnets are held close together. After eliminating a variety of possibilities—and impossibilities—Hill concludes that the only type of repulsive force field that could account for the known interactions of these objects with vehicles (stoppages), tree limbs (broken), and water (disturbed), is a gravity canceling field of some kind.

This mode of propulsion would neatly resolve a number of puzzling problems surrounding the UFO mystery. For one, it allows the occupants of a craft propelled in this fashion to survive extreme accelerations without high onboard g forces. It would also permit supersonic flight through the atmosphere without sonic booms. And it would eliminate the high aerodynamic heating that plagues the space shuttle, for example, and requires the use of special heat-resistant tiles over portions of its fuselage.

As part of the gravity canceling propulsive field package, a sheath of ionized and excited air molecules called a plasma would surround the craft. Such a sheath would affect a variety of observables, such as the craft's color during various phases of its flight—red and orange during hovering and slow motions, blue and white at, or in expectation of, high speeds—as well as how sharp or blurry its edges appear at night, even its overall shape. In fact, when police officers Dale Spaur and Wilber Neff reported seeing an "ice cream cone" shaped object over Ohio in 1966 (see page 114), it's likely what they saw, according to Hill, was an opaque plasma cone below a rising, domed saucer.

Hill's most welcome conclusion is that a UFO weighing in at about thirty tons, capable of 100g accelerations and speeds of 9,000 mph in the atmosphere, would actually be obeying, rather than defying, the laws of physics and engineering. Just how one could achieve such a gravity canceling propulsive field is, of course, beyond Hill—and beyond us. Otherwise, we would all be driving classic flying saucers to work instead of Chevy Suburbans and Mazda Miatas.

WAVES AND FLAPS

What just about anyone with an interest in this subject wants to know, of course, is just when and where UFOs are most likely to be seen. Periods of high UFO activity are known as "flaps" or "waves." UFO historian Jerome Clark in his UFO encyclopedia defines a UFO flap or wave in the broadest sense as "any noticeable rise in UFO reports above the usual rate." Captain Edward J.

Ruppelt, a former director of the Air Force's Project Blue Book, whose job was to investigate such flaps, somewhat more colorfully defined them as "a condition or situation, or state of being of a group characterized by an advanced degree of confusion that has not yet reached panic proportions."

But the controversy about flaps and waves has always been over the issue of whether or not they represent a real increase in the actual number of UFOs present at any given time, or merely reflect increased publicity. It's the UFO version of the chicken and egg conundrum. Which comes first, the UFOs or the media attention that supposedly predisposes more people to see—and report—UFOs where there are none? In a trenchant, award-winning analysis published in *The Anomalist,* researcher Martin Kottmeyer demonstrated, contrary to the claims of the debunkers, that "peak media coverage . . . lags behind peak UFO numbers."

Historians of this subject recognize prominent post-Arnold waves, including the years 1947, 1952, 1954, 1957, 1966, and 1973. Other historical dates have also been put forth as Flap Years, but these are largely contingent on how broadly one wants to define the UFO phenomenon itself. Did it begin with Arnold, so to speak, or has it always been with us, in one permutation or another?

For instance, beginning in November 1896, and continuing until May of the following year (with a peak in April), American newspapers ran literally hundreds of articles reporting the appearance of a large, unidentified "airship"—six years before Kitty Hawk and the Wright brothers. But this was also during the age of so-called "yellow journalism," a time when both reporters and editors weren't above creating stories out of whole cloth when news was slow. Although opinion remains divided, we tend to come down on the side of the argument that says the Great Airship was a widespread hoax perpetrated on the American reading public as newspapers competed to outdo one another, though there may well have been a *few* genuine UFO reports during this time.

More problematic is a series of sightings centered around two small villages in Wales, Barmouth and Harlech, that took place in the years 1904–1905. The lights, which coincided with a local religious revival and were seen by hundreds, including reporters for the *Daily Mail,* were described as yellow balls of light of "electric vividness." English researcher Paul Devereux and others have attributed the Wales wave to earthlights—a natural phenomena associated with the tectonic strain that also generates earth tremors.

In 1909 a UFO wave crashed up against England's eastern coastline, where reports proliferated of torpedo-shaped objects bearing "searchlights" and making engine noises in the night. The "Zeppelin scare" repeated itself over England at the end of 1912 and into 1913. Both incidents have often been attributed to "war nerves" preceding the outbreak of the First World War.

Between the years 1933 and 1938 hundreds of Scandinavians reported a large gray airplane with no insignia that flew very close to the ground at night and also shone bright searchlights. The "ghost flier," as it became known, frequently flew in heavy fog and during blizzards—conditions that would have grounded most airplanes of the day. In the summer of 1946 the same Scandinavian countries would be the site of another UFO flap. This time the objects were referred to in the press as "ghost rockets." They were called "rockets" because of their torpedo shapes, and "ghost" because, like the phantom flier of a decade earlier, their provenance was never conclusively determined.

Kenneth Arnold's sighting of a "flying saucer" changed everything. Unlike previously, UFOs have been continuously reported ever since, beginning with the summer 1947 wave unleashed by his report. The next major flap occurred in the United States during the summer of 1952, with reports following worldwide. This was the wave that included radar/visual sightings over Washington National Airport on two consecutive weekends in late July, resulting in the largest Pentagon press conference since the end of the Second World War. It also resulted, the following year, in the CIA-sponsored Robertson Panel.

The first flap to overlook North America and occur entirely abroad took place during September through November 1954. Activity centered in both South America and Europe, but clustered especially in France and Italy. What was so remarkable about the third modern wave was that such a large percentage of the French cases reported humanoidlike entities in association with landed UFOs. For the first time, UFO groups were forced to consider such reports seriously.

In November 1957 the UFOs were back over the U.S. with a vengeance. One of the most spectacular sightings of the 1957 wave involved a series of sightings by multiple independent witnesses near the small Texas town of Levelland (see page 74). Several of these witnesses reported headlight and engine failure while in proximity to a large, egg-shaped UFO, with both systems returning to normal operation once the UFO departed.

The famous 1966 wave actually began in the fall of 1965 with a spate of sightings over Exeter, New Hampshire. By the spring of 1966 strange objects were being reported over Michigan. The Air Force tried to explain away these sightings as "swamp gas" but made a laughingstock of themselves in the process. As a result, both the press and politicians began taking UFOs more seriously than ever before, which provided a welcome platform for a number of other high profile cases that occurred across the United States that year.

In October 1973 an extensive UFO flap again rattled the U.S. The most dramatic incident happened on the evening of October 11, when two Mississippi fishermen, Charles Hickson and Calvin Parker, claimed they were transported inside a UFO, examined, and released in Pascagoula. Wave activity continued in Australia and Europe into 1974. The autumn of 1978 saw another flap over Italy, Australia, and South America. Canada and the Soviet Union experienced their own dramatic increases in UFO sightings in the autumn and winter of 1989. Finally, a spectacular wave struck Belgium late in the same year and continued over into 1990. The Belgian wave was characterized by reports of huge, triangle-shaped objects, often flying silently at low speeds and altitudes.

Miniflaps—waves of reports confined to a localized area or community—have occurred numerous times in UFO history, far too often to mention, in fact. By way of a single example, a miniflap occurred over the Hudson Valley area of New York in the mid-1980s, in which more than 5,000 people reportedly saw a huge triangular-shaped UFO.

Despite years worth of data, attempts to predict UFO waves by proponents have for the most part been spectacularly unsuccessful. One of the earliest post-1947 theories tried to draw a connection between the closest approach of the planet Mars to Earth with a seasonal proliferation of UFO reports, but subsequent data derailed this train of thought almost as soon as it pulled out of the station. Skeptics have fared little better. Their prediction that UFO sightings would soar in 1977 in the wake of the release of Steven Spielberg's blockbuster movie, *Close Encounters of the Third Kind,* died on arrival as well. After a half century of UFO reports, all that can be ascertained with certainty is that no one knows when the next UFO sighting will occur.

HOT SPOTS

If not in time, could any prediction be made about *where* the next UFO sighting will take place? Some ufologists have tried to narrow the would-be observer's odds by identifying what they refer to as UFO "windows" and "hot spots." Whereas "flaps" designate a *time* period when an increase in UFO activity takes place, "windows" represent *places* where UFO activity occurs from time to time. But unlike "window" areas, which can open and close, "hot spots" are places where UFOs seem to be reported rather steadily over time—it's a fine line between the two terms, however, and many use them interchangeably. But as a rule of thumb, waves move around, windows tend to stay put but are occasional, while hot spots are areas of more or less constant activity.

The very concept of window areas remains a contentious one among ufologists, however. It was originally proposed as a portal or opening to another world or dimension, a region where, for whatever reason(s), access between the two worlds was somehow facilitated. That UFOs could be thought of in interdimensional terms in the first place arose out of the failure of the

Extraterrestrial Hypothesis (ETH) of UFO origins to account for all of the reported behavior of UFOs. The ETH seemed reasonable enough when it posited physical objects piloted by physical beings. But then UFOs began behaving in most unseemly, unphysical ways, sometimes materializing out of thin air, other times disappearing into it. They seemed capable of changing shape almost at will. Inexplicably, they also seemed to favor certain places over time with their presence. And so it was that the notion of UFO "hot spots" took hold.

Five places in the United States can lay claim to being UFO hot spots:

Gulf Breeze, Florida, located near Eglin Air Force Base and the Naval Air Station in Pensacola, has been a major UFO hot spot for well over a decade. Some identify the window area as ranging from the Florida panhandle in the east, to coastal Alabama and west to Mississippi, where two men fishing in Pascagoula were abducted by wrinkled-skinned creatures in the fall of 1973, making national headlines. But the person who put Gulf Breeze itself on everyone's UFO map was a local businessman by the name of Ed Walters. On November 11, 1987, Walters took the first in a long series of photographs and films of a glowing object shaped somewhat like a Chinese lamp shade with portholes. While some ufologists have analyzed the Walters photographs and pronounced them genuine, others have uncovered evidence of models and other kinds of trickery. Whatever the merits or demerits of the Walters case, numerous other witnesses in the area have reported similar sightings on countless occasions ever since. In late January 1998, for instance, a dozen skywatchers gathered on Pensacola Beach were treated to the sight of a cherry-red luminous object that stopped and started repeatedly and took a very unairplanelike angled turn. This red object is seen so frequently by area residents that they have affectionately named it "Bubba."

Pine Bush, New York, is a tiny hamlet of about 2,000 people located eighty miles north of New York City, and not far from where Whitley Strieber's UFO experiences, recounted in the best-selling book *Communion,* took place. Since the 1980s the area has been a mecca for UFO seekers, though policemen, store clerks, and other working-class citizens have reported seeing UFOs here since about 1969. One of these seekers, musician Ellen Crystal, has taken so many photographs (about 1,500) of "spaceships" (and two of humanoid figures) since she first came to Pine Bush in 1980 that her name is virtually synonymous with this otherwise sleepy little town. She claims to have seen a variety of craft in the area, including the "triangle" and the "boomerang," as well as the "diamond," the "manta ray," and the "walnut" or "turtle." Geologist Bruce Cornet, who has also seen and photographed the objects, is convinced these objects with their zigzags, tiny loops, and midair stops cannot possibly be conventional airplanes. But of late the locals have not taken kindly to all the skywatching by outsiders on West Searesville Road, and Orange County is making an effort to ban the practice! From Pine Bush, of course, it's just a short hop and skip across the Hudson River to the scene of the famous Hudson Valley sightings of the 1980s, an area that UFO investigator Philip Imbrogno believes has one of the highest incidences of reported UFO sightings in the world.

Rachel, Nevada, population 100, is home to the infamous Little A-Le-Inn and sits just outside the northern boundary of one of the country's most secret and closely guarded sites—an unacknowledged air base that goes by the name of Groom Lake, aka Dreamland, or Area 51. The U-2 spy plane flew here, as did its successor, the SR-71 Blackbird, and the F-117 Stealth fighter, while all were still under official wraps. Just to the southwest, at the Nevada Test Site, is where most of our Cold War nuclear bomb tests were carried out, far from prying eyes. But it was also at Area 51, in 1989, that uncredentialed physicist Bob Lazar claimed to have helped reverse-engineer a captured flying saucer, setting off a spate of sightings of unusual lights and objects that continue to this day. The overwhelming majority of these sightings are no doubt attributable to military technology in the form of flare drops and advanced aircraft flights. But shape-shifting UFOs (in one case allegedly disguised as an automobile!) and abductions have also been reported in the immediate vicinity of Rachel and Area 51. Most watchers gather at the so-called Black Mailbox nineteen miles south of town. In April 1996, in association with publicity surrounding the movie *Independence Day*, then Nevada Governor Bob Miller declared Highway 375, which runs through Rachel, north of Las Vegas, "The Extraterrestrial Highway."

The San Luis Valley is the world's largest alpine valley. Forty-five miles wide, 120 miles long, it stretches from south-central Colorado into northern New Mexico. It was here, on September 7, 1967, that an Appaloosa filly named Lady (and erroneously reported as Snippy) was found mutilated, her entire neck and head stripped of flesh. A wave of animal mutilation reports followed, leading to a 1979 investigation by a retired FBI agent, Kenneth Rommel, which concluded that predators were responsible. But mutilation reports continue in the San Luis Valley today (as well as in other remote areas of the country), frequently in association with sightings of so-called black helicopters and UFOs, the latter largely of the colored, nocturnal ball of light variety. Christopher O'Brien, now a resident of the area and author of *The Mysterious Valley* and a follow-up volume, serves as a clearinghouse for such stories and maintains a site devoted to them on the web.

Yakima, Washington, has an airport where Kenneth Arnold landed just after his June 24, 1947, "flying saucer" sighting that set off the UFO mystery. But a variety of UFOs have been seen at the Yakima Indian reservation in south-central Washington State both before, according to Yakima Indian legends, and since Arnold's famous sighting. In March 1952, for instance, radar at McChord Air Force Base picked up an unidentified target west of Yakima; the pilot of the scrambled F-94 witnessed a large "ball of fire" for forty-five seconds. But since the mid-1960s, and in particular the 1970s, there have been hundreds of reports of unexplained lights and objects in the area, many of which were originally gathered by the local fire control officer, William Vogel, and his fire lookout crew, police, and other investigators. Until his death in 1985, Vogel collected reports of objects with multicolored lights, daylight discs, and objects chasing aircraft and automobiles. Particular attention was paid the phenomenon between 1972 and 1973, when Seattle engineer David Akers, using a variety of high-tech equipment, regularly observed and photographed mystery lights that could not be "readily explained by known causes." Most were nocturnal lights, generally bright and larger than a point source, usually orange-colored, and often moving in such a way as to "give the appearance of intelligent control." Researcher Greg Long wrote the definite account of sightings in the area, *Examining the Earthlight Theory: The Yakima UFO Microcosm,* in 1990. Reports continue to come from Yakima, but given its location in an Indian reservation, observers need special permission to skywatch from the area.

But even if you don't have the time, money, or inclination to travel across the country to visit one of these UFO hot spots, you might still be able to improve your chances by going to the hottest spot within your own state. We asked Joseph Trainor, editor of *UFO Roundup,* a weekly Internet UFO newsletter that keeps its finger on the pulse of the subject, to provide us with a list of cities/towns that serve, as he put it, as the "saucer capital" of each of the fifty states. These are the communities which, according to Trainor's seat-of-the-pants survey, have the highest incidence of UFO sightings.

Without further ado then, here's the list:

STATE	CITY/TOWN
Alabama	Huntsville
Alaska	Palmer
Arizona	Tucson
Arkansas	Hot Springs
California	San Bernardino
Colorado	Salida

STATE	CITY/TOWN
Connecticut	Willimantic
Delaware	Dover
Florida	Pensacola
Georgia	LaGrange
Hawaii	Kailua Kona
Idaho	Pocatello
Illinois	Naperville
Indiana	Bloomington
Iowa	Lewiston
Kansas	Wichita
Kentucky	Hopkinsville
Louisiana	New Orleans
Maine	Augusta
Maryland	Lexington Park
Massachusetts	Fitchburg
Michigan	Benton Harbor
Minnesota	Mankato
Mississippi	Meridian
Missouri	Springfield
Montana	Great Falls
Nebraska	Lincoln
Nevada	Rachel
New Hampshire	Portsmouth
New Jersey	Atlantic City
New Mexico	Taos
New York	Newburgh
North Carolina	Salisbury
North Dakota	Devil's Lake
Ohio	Owensville
Oklahoma	Enid
Oregon	Klamath Falls
Pennsylvania	Scranton
Rhode Island	South Kingstown
South Carolina	Columbia
South Dakota	Rapid City
Tennessee	Gatlinburg

STATE	CITY/TOWN
Texas	Arlington
Utah	Provo
Vermont	White River Junction
Virginia	Richmond
Washington	Spokane
West Virginia	Sistersville
Wisconsin	Green Bay
Wyoming	Gillette

Of course, UFO hot spots occur outside the United States, as well. English researcher Jenny Randles, notes the following among the more well-known foreign windows.

The *Hessdalen Valley* in central *Norway* has probably produced more UFO pictures than any other hot spot in the world, with the exception of Gulf Breeze. The UFOs seen here are invariably blobs of white, orange, or blue lights. Most are solitary performers, but occasionally a string of such lights will appear, giving the appearance that they are attached to a structured object. While the balls of light were known locally since at least 1944, they only came to the attention of the public at large following a series of early 1982 sightings. The following year, UFO groups from Norway and Sweden launched Project Hessdalen, a coordinated five-week study of the phenomenon that resulted in 188 individual sightings, supported by photographic and other instrumentation. Unfortunately for the would-be investigators, the Hessdalen lights typically appear in the winter months, when temperatures routinely drop to minus thirty degrees centigrade.

The *Pennine Hills,* on the border between Lancashire and Yorkshire, is *England*'s most consistent hot spot. Reports of ghost lights stretch back at least two centuries. In this century, the area has seen more than its fair share of close encounters and abductions, beginning with a 1914 sighting of the so-called British Airship. On March 9, 1977, two factory workers were startled by a multicolored object that fell out of the clouds and stalled their car engine, cutting off the lights. In November 1980, near Todmorden, police officer Alan Godfrey reported ten minutes of missing time after an oval, rotating mass blocked the road in front of his patrol car, leaving a "swirled circle" on the wet pavement. The best place to look for UFOs is said to be an abandoned quarry near the small community of Stacksteads.

The huge and largely uninhabited **Nullarbor Plain** of south **Australia** stretches along the Indian Ocean, between Perth and Adelaide, for hundreds of miles. So unpopulated is the area that the British tested their nuclear weapons here in the 1950s, near Maralinga. In November 1957, during a major UFO flap, a group of people driving on the Eyre Highway saw a silver disc hover directly over the bomb site for fifteen minutes, before it finally shot straight up and disappeared. Plates and windows could be clearly seen on the side of the disc. On the evening of February 4, 1973, a nurse and her boyfriend encountered a rectangular orange glow beside the road, in which a white humanoid figure seemed to be standing. An even more terrifying encounter occurred on January 21, 1988 (See page 80), when an entire family claimed their car was "attacked" and lifted into the air by a UFO shaped like an oval egg with an egg-cup base. A highway sign "warning" of UFO road hazards now marks the spot.

Halfway around the world, the much smaller Caribbean island of **Puerto Rico** has also been a rich source of UFO reports—as well as a few sensational hoaxes. A local wave swept the capital city, San Juan, in 1973, followed two years later by widespread reports of animal mutilations, which continue to this day. UFOs have been reported entering and leaving lakes, and a number of underground bases in association with UFOs have also been claimed. Puerto Rico's unique contribution to the literature of the odd and unusual is undoubtedly the *chupacabras*—or "goat sucker"—a small, hairy, red-eyed creature accused of draining blood from its victims, mostly small animals in the form of goats and chickens. But its association with UFOs is tenuous at best.

South America's UFO hot spot is concentrated in, but not limited to, the state of **Rio Grande do Norte** in **Brazil**'s most northeastern corner. Reporter Bob Pratt, who has made six field trips to the area, collected enough cases to fill an entire book. Many of the reported UFOs are rectangular in shape, like an upright flying refrigerator, and often emit beams of powerful light. What's most unusual about the Brazilian cases, however, is the large number of humans apparently targeted by the phenomenon. Victims report being chased, pulled into the air and dropped. Others claim to have been burned by the light beams, and at least a handful of deaths have been blamed on UFOs. This hot spot is definitely not for the faint of heart.

IN THEORY

Many UFO hot spots are characterized by a particular type of UFO, usually balls of light, which suggests that many may have the same explanation. Is it possible to arrive at a UFO theory (or theories) using the form of the UFO as the foremost consideration? We believe it is. At least that is the premise of our book.

While existing UFO theories are almost as numerous as the reported shapes, most serious hypotheses fall into one of the following categories:

Terrestrial Manufacture: This would include claims of Nazi or other current but secret man-made technology perceived as UFOs.

Natural Phenomena: The least exotic of these suggests that UFOs may indeed be of a terrestrial or atmospheric origin, but one wholly natural. Prime candidates include ball lightning and so-called "earthlights." Unfortunately, the mechanism of these two arguably interrelated phenomena are almost as little understood as the UFO itself. The most exotic of the natural explanations is the Tectonic Strain theory promoted by Canadian neurophysiologist Michael Persinger. Persinger posits that energy fluctuations generated by fault lines are capable of interacting with the human nervous system, specifically with the brain's temporal lobe. While the Earth strain hypothesis permits some UFOs to be visible as BOLs (balls of light), follow-up encounters, say, with UFO occupants or abductors, are viewed as a sort of planet-induced hallucination.

Time-Travelers. UFOs are perceived as time machines (either terrestrial or extraterrestrial) from the future. This would theoretically "explain" their ability to pop in and out of view at a moment's notice. It might also account for the humanoid appearance of the reported occupants, i.e., they look like us because they *are* us.

Extraterrestrial: The so-called ETH, or Extraterrestrial Hypothesis, posits that flying saucers and UFOs are space vehicles from another planet, and their occupants biological life-forms with a different evolutionary history than that of *Homo sapiens*; in other words, true extraterrestrials.

Interdimensional: This differs from the Time Travel hypothesis in that it theorizes UFOs from another physical dimension. In other words, instead of coming from another *time,* UFOs are seen as arriving from another *place* in a parallel time.

Imaginal: This term applies to the imagination as a literal *realm,* in which images and entities exist as physical facts on par with the features (or phenomena) of the natural landscape. It is significantly distinct from saying that UFOs are merely products or by-products of the human imagination and nervous system—misperceptions, hallucinations, hoaxes, sensations generated during sensory states of sleep paralysis and other altered states of consciousness, and so on.

These six explanations barely scrape the surface of UFO theories. Unfortunately for the promoters of other theories, however, few have much in the way of evidence, beyond the scattered anecdote, to support their case. For example, Arnold himself, as a consequence of having seen a transparent UFO, eventually came to believe that they were living creatures who inhabited the atmosphere, just as jellyfish do the oceans.

The most fervent promoter of the space "critter" theory was Trevor James Constable, an aviation historian and student of the teachings of Wilhelm J. Reich, the father of "orgone" energy. Constable promoted his critter hypothesis, accompanied by a series of photographs (mostly taken with infrared film) in a pair of books. To Constable's mind, UFOs, which could be seen by the unaided eye only under certain conditions, were single-cell organisms, aerial amoebas, as it were, which he called "bioforms." Constable's ideas were heavily influenced by those of Reich, who saw Earth as a battlefield between malignant and benign UFOs. The former gave off negative orgone, resulting in our planet's growing deserts. But the dearth of data in support of the critter hypothesis suggests it is more a theory in search of a body of evidence rather than the other way around.

Other theories put forth for UFO propagation include projected holographic images (a sort of Cold War psychological warfare experiment), heavenly messengers (both angelic and demonic), unknown and unidentified Earth energies associated with ley lines or Gaia grids, ancient astronauts (as opposed to future ones), plasma vortices (also perhaps responsible for crop circles), astronomical mirages, mass hysteria, a civilization inhabiting the inside of a hollow Earth (or the far side of the moon, or even—shades of Atlantis!—the ocean floor), and so on. In common with the critter hypothesis, these, too, seem to be ideas in search of convincing evidence which have come up lacking. With the possible exception of spinning plasmas, such theories have virtually nothing to address or add to the issue of UFO *form*. Nor can form tell us anything about possible origins in such instances.

Numerous witnesses have reported a seemingly structured flying disc capable of either entering or exiting bodies of water, for example, as well as flying with equal ease through the air. But unless further evidence of actual origin is forthcoming, it is impossible to conclude, or even suggest, anything about its ultimate origins. Did it enter in and out of a dome-covered city on the sea floor, or through some underwater passage leading to the center of a hollow Earth, or are air and water merely one and the same medium to someone else's highly advanced technology?

THE ANSWER(S)

As we have seen, UFOs come in an abundant, mind-boggling proliferation of shapes, from light forms to gigantic saucers, cigars, wedges and flying wings. Coupled with the staggering number of UFO reports, it seems safe to say, on the surface, that not every UFO can be an extraterrestrial spaceship. For starters, we know that well over ninety percent of all UFOs are misidentified mundane and natural phenomena. The real question is, can *any* UFO be of extraterrestrial or otherwise extraordinary origin? We believe the answer is yes.

While the weird world of quantum mechanics offers suggestive hints of such future possibilities as time, faster-than-light, and interdimensional travel, it's effectively impossible at this point to relate such cutting edge notions to basic UFO form. What would be the "best" shape for a time machine, for example? Who's to say that a sleek, circular disc is any more organic or suited to the requirements necessitated by time travel than a perfect sphere, say, or Dr. Who's telegenic red telephone booth?

Moreover, given the confusing variety of UFO shapes reported, we are faced with the same conundrum that confronts the ET hypothesis. Just as *all* UFOs can't conceivably be extraterrestrial visitors, it seems unlikely they can all be time machines or interdimensional devices, either—unless both space and the future are much more crowded than the current evidence suggests.

Left with a conservative approach to the form versus theory problem, then, we propose the following.

Small, dim, amorphous blobs or balls of light seen by night are most probably of terrestrial origin. The most likely candidate in such cases would seem to be ball lightning or some other type of little understood atmospheric plasma, or ionized gas. While we realize this hovers perilously close to explaining one mystery by resorting to another, we feel the theory best fits the facts. There's no compelling reason, for example, to either assume or postulate that simple balls of light represent anything remotely resembling advanced technology in the form of space, time, or interdimensional travel. Balls of light (BOLs) are probably just what they appear to be, and nothing more. Shaving the now hoary, Rumplestiltskinlike UFO beard with Ockham's most excellent (if not necessarily infallible) razor, this would lead us to preclude BOLs as robotic probes emitted by larger, parent UFOs.

Why would remote sensors need to *glow*, in other words, when such an activity would arguably interfere with its own information-gathering capabilities?

Nocturnal light *formations* are more problematic. If one assumes that they simply represent a collection of balls of light like the above, one must then explain the seeming necessary intelligence to form a formation. However, geese fly in formation, but it would be hard to argue that they do so out of intelligence, or conscious, directed choice. Instead it seems reasonable to suppose that if one ball of light can form under certain specific conditions, why not several or many? And as one behaves as a result of existing conditions—prevailing wind, electrical differentials, and so on—why not the many?

Again, while we may be accused of taking the path of least resistance, there is no compelling evidence that light formations, in and of themselves, argue for a necessarily technological or other nonordinary origin. A time machine would have no intrinsic need to be outlined in lights, for example, and for that matter, neither would an alien spacecraft. (Why UFOs have lights at all is a matter of minor debate within the UFO community.) In the same vein, the human witness, observing a geometrical pattern of lights against a dark background, is probably perceptually compelled, even justified, to "add" a framing structure for the lights.

Nocturnal light arrangements that consist of both a bright point source and a visible directed beam are admittedly a different matter altogether. We feel safe in saying that such cases are obviously outside the realm of a natural phenomenon, however broadly defined or previously unreported and unrecognized. Still, a formation of lights seen at night does not allow us to conclude much about the object to which they are apparently attached. Nothing in their nature is necessarily extraterrestrial or dimensional. However unlikely, they could represent terrestrial military technology, or—in rarer cases—elaborate hoaxes.

Conversely, they could also represent the real thing, as seen by night, although no one has ever arrived at a satisfactory explanation as to why any UFO would require so many darn bright lights in the first place. Or why they would require illumination for any purpose. Given that we have night-vision goggles and other light-enhancing devices, it seems absurd to postulate aliens who upon arrival, having conquered the immense distances of space travel, still lag behind twentieth century terrestrial technology in terms of turning night into day. Arguments that UFOs display lights simply to be seen strike us as circular reasoning in the extreme, a case of the conclusion outrunning the horse that is supposedly carting it.

Daylight discs, spheres, cigars, and ovals we find even more difficult to dismiss, while admitting they suffer from the same embarrassment of riches as do the nocturnal light cases. Why should alien spaceships come in such confusing, multivaried forms? Standing on the outskirts of a major Earth city and noting the many design differences of the various cars, trucks, and vans as they drive down the freeway is one thing; imagining that our home planet is little more than a rest stop or airport hub on some intergalactic autobahn—visited now by a Ford Explorer equivalent from Zeta Reticuli, next by a convertible Pleiadean BMW with the top momentarily down—is to strain both science and credulity. Such a reality would also lay to rest most UFO conspiracy theories by definition. Given such a volume of daily and nightly extraterrestrial traffic, how could *any* government or intelligence agency hope to keep the influx of that many ET tourists a closely guarded secret? The fact of the matter is that they couldn't—even if they wanted to.

At the same time, we find ourselves running out of reasoning room. Unless each and every one of our case witnesses is to be dismissed on grounds of delusional or other inherent tendencies or traits, a clear, core pattern emerges of an object changing both over time and circumstance. That is, in general, the lower to the ground and the closer to the witnesses, the more add-ons or appurtenances are reported. Put another way, more details emerge even as the essential underlying form may differ in basic geometrical fundamentals. And those fundamentals, from disc and sphere to cigar, as we've seen, may very well depend on such peripheral or secondary factors as the angle and duration of observation, including the object's actual behavior.

This is the same pattern one would expect of a terrestrial object like a jet fighter or aircraft carrier when viewed close up, rather than at distances of thousands of feet, or tens of miles. It is decidedly not the same pattern of perception one would anticipate of a circular ball of light, for example, unless the latter were obscured here and there by clouds or trees, or affected by other circumstances. Theoretically, the closer one got to a ball of light, the more one would expect it to resemble same, although internal details might become more apparent. Certainly the last thing one would anticipate would be a BOL—or mirage—suddenly sprouting antennas, flanges, and/or "landing" legs, let alone disgorging seemingly humanoidlike figures.

Followed to its logical conclusion, this strain of thought leads us to believe that a tiny percentage of UFO cases may very well be the real thing—evidence of a technologically advanced craft manufactured by someone, either not of this Earth, time, or dimension. Extraterrestrial? Perhaps, though there is no solid evidence to support such a conclusion. Time or dimensional travelers? Who can say? But it's quite clear that their visits—whoever *they* might be—are extremely rare, certainly nothing like the frequency of an airline shuttle. It's by no means a daily occurrence, unlike what most UFO buffs would have us believe. And it's not likely weekly or monthly, either. We are talking perhaps a few times per year, roughly equivalent to the flights of our own space shuttle. At least that would make sense—or as much sense as anything about this puzzling subject ever does.

So we've got visitors. Does anybody care?

ACKNOWLEDGMENTS

The authors would like to thank the following people for their help, suggestions, or inspiration in the production of this book: Larry W. Bryant, Peter Brookesmith, Jerry Clark, Loren Coleman, Tom Deuley, Paul Devereux, Hilary Evans, Richard H. Hall, Antonio Huneeus, Karl Pflock, and Joseph Trainor.

BIBLIOGRAPHY

(These references primarily support the book's Introduction and Afterword, though they served as well to supplement the specific sources listed in the Field Guide descriptions.)

Arnold, Kenneth and Ray Palmer. *The Coming of the Saucers: A Documentary Report on Sky Objects That Have Mystified the World.* Boise, Idaho, and Amherst, Wisconsin: the Authors, 1952.

Bethurum, Truman. *Aboard a Flying Saucer.* Los Angeles: DeVorss & Co., 1954.

Brookesmith, Peter. *UFO: The Complete Sightings.* New York: Barnes & Noble, 1995.

Bullard, Thomas E. *UFO Abductions: The Measure of a Mystery. Vol. 1 Comparative Study of Abduction Reports.* Mount Rainier, Maryland: Fund for UFO Research, 1987.

Clark, Jerome. *UFOs in the 1980s: The UFO Encyclopedia, Vol. 1.* Detroit: Omnigraphics, 1990.

Clark, Jerome. *The Emergence of a Phenomenon: UFOs from the Beginning through 1959, The UFO Encyclopedia, Vol. 2.* Detroit: Omnigraphics, 1992.

Clark, Jerome. *High Strangeness: UFOs from 1960 through 1979, The UFO Encyclopedia, Vol. 3.* Detroit: Omnigraphics, 1996.

Clarke, David and Andy Roberts. *Phantoms of the Sky.* London: Robert Hale, 1990.

Constable, Trevor James. *The Cosmic Pulse of Life.* Garberville, California: Borderland Sciences, 1990.

Constable, Trevor James. *They Live in the Sky.* Los Angeles: New Age Publishing Co., 1959.

Crystal, Ellen. *Silent Invasion: The Shocking Discoveries of a UFO Researcher.* New York: Paragon House, 1991.

Evans, Hilary and John Spencer (eds.). *UFOs 1947–1987: The 40-Year Search for an Explanation.* London: Fortean Tomes, 1987.

Evans, Hilary and Dennis Stacy (eds.). *UFOs 1947–1997: Fifty Years of Flying Saucers.* London: John Brown Publishing, 1997.

Fuller, John. *The Interrupted Journey: Two Lost Hours "Aboard A Flying Saucer."* New York: Dial, 1966.

Fry, Daniel. *The White Sands Incident.* Los Angeles: New Age Publishing Co., 1954.

Gillmor, Daniel S. (ed.). *Scientific Study of Unidentified Flying Objects.* New York: Bantam, 1969.

Hall, Richard H. (ed.). *The UFO Evidence.* Washington, D.C.: National Investigations Committee on Aerial Phenomena, 1964.

Hall, Richard H. *The UFO Evidence: Volume II.* unpublished.

Hazelwood, Lynn. "Strangeness in the Night," *Hudson Valley,* October 1997.

Hill, Paul R. *Unconventional Flying Objects: A Scientific Analysis.* Charlottesville, Virginia: Hampton Roads Publishing, 1995.

Huneeus, Antonio. *UFO: 1998 Calendar.* New York: Stewart Tabori & Chang, 1997.

Huyghe, Patrick. "U.F.O. Files: The Untold Story," *The New York Times Magazine,* October 14, 1979.

Huyghe, Patrick. "Scientists Who Have Seen UFOs," *Science Digest,* November 1981.

Huyghe, Patrick. "The Secret Invasion: Does It Add Up?" *Omni,* Winter 1995.

Hynek, J. Allen. *The UFO Experience: A Scientific Inquiry.* Chicago: Regnery, 1972.

Hynek, J. Allen and Philip J. Imbrogno with Bob Pratt. *Night Siege: The Hudson Valley UFO Sightings.* New York: Ballantine, 1987.

Jacobs, David M. *The Threat.* New York: Simon & Schuster, 1998.

Kottmeyer, Martin. "UFO Flaps," *The Anomalist: 3* (Winter 1995–96).

Kulikowski II, Stan. "Infernal UFOs: Bigger Inside Than Out?" *MUFON UFO Journal, No. 313* (May 1994).

Lindeman, Michael. "New UFO Wave in Florida Panhandle, South Alabama," *CNI News,* 3:24, February 16, 1998.

Long, Greg. *Examining the Earthlight Theory: The Yakima UFO Microcosm.* Evanston, Illinois: Center for UFO Studies, 1990.

Maccabee, Bruce. "Acceleration," *MUFON 1996 International UFO Symposium Proceedings.* Sequin, Texas: MUFON, 1996.

McCarthy, Paul. "Tour of a UFO," *Omni,* December 1990.

Mesnard, Joel. "The French Abduction File," *MUFON UFO Journal, No. 309* (January 1994).

O'Brien, Christopher. *The Mysterious Valley.* New York: St. Martin's Paperbacks, 1996.

Pflock, Karl T. "UFOs: For RAND Use Only," *The Anomalist: 5* (Summer 1997).

Powers, W. T. "The Landing at Socorro," *The Humanoids,* Charles Bowen (ed.). London: Futura, 1974.

Pratt, Bob. *UFO Danger Zone.* Madison, Wisconsin: Horus House Press, 1996.

Quintanilla, Hector J. "Project Blue Book's Last Years," *The Anomalist: 4* (Autumn 1996).

Randles, Jenny. *UFOs and How to See Them*. New York: Barnes & Noble, 1997.

Ruppelt, Edward J. *The Report on Unidentified Flying Objects*. New York, Ace, 1956.

Salisbury, Frank B. *The Utah UFO Display: A Biologist's Report*. Old Greenwich, Connecticut: Devin-Adair, 1974.

Sanderson, Ivan T. *Invisible Residents*. New York: World Publishing, 1970.

Sheffield, Derek. *UFO: A Deadly Concealment*. London: Blandford, 1996.

Stacy, Dennis. "Cosmic Conspiracy: Six Decades of Government UFO Cover-ups," *Omni,* April–September, 1994.

Stacy, Dennis. "Crop Circles," *Encyclopedia of Strange and Unexplained Physical Phenomena,* Jerome Clark (ed.). Detroit: Gale, 1993.

Stacy, Dennis. "When Pilots See UFOs," *Smithsonian Air & Space,* December 1987/January 1988.

Story, Ronald. D. *The Encyclopedia of UFOs*. New York: Doubleday, 1980.

Strieber Whitley. *Communion: A True Story*. New York: Beech Tree Books, 1987.

Vallee, Jacques and Janine. *Challenge to Science: The UFO Enigma*. New York: Ace Books, 1966.

Vallee, Jacques. *Confrontations: A Scientist's Search for Alien Contact*. New York: Ballantine Books, 1990.

RESOURCES

The best way to keep up with current UFO activity is through the Internet. There are thousands of UFO-related sites on the net, but most, unfortunately, are of dubious quality. We recommend Peter Davenport's National UFO Reporting Center, which is just what it claims to be. The NUFORC site is located at *http://www.ufocenter.com*. If you wish to report a *recent* UFO sighting, you can call it in to them at (206) 722-3000. Glen Campbell's huge, no frills site Ufomind, also known as the Mothership, can be found at *http://www.ufomind.com*. Another excellent website for UFO information is UFO city at *http://www.ufocity.com*. You'll find lots of useful resources here, including links to UFO organizations worldwide.

The "world's largest UFO membership organization," if you're interested, is MUFON, the Mutual UFO Network. MUFON trains UFO field investigators, publishes a comprehensive UFO investigations guide, sponsors an annual UFO Symposium, and issues the monthly *MUFON UFO Journal*. Membership is $30 a year. Contact: MUFON, 103 Oldtowne Road, Seguin, TX 78155-4099. Phone: (830) 379-9216. Or catch them on the web at *http://mufon.com* or *http://www.rutgers.edu/~mcgrew/ MUFON*.

The J. Allen Hynek Center for UFO Studies (*http://www.cufos.org*) publishes a quarterly journal, the *International UFO Reporter*, and the annual *Journal of UFO Studies*. The CUFOS address is: 2457 W. Peterson Avenue, Chicago, IL 60659. The Fund for UFO Research supplies financial assistance to approved research projects and then publishes the results. More information can be found at *http://www.fufor.org* or write to them at: FUFOR, P.O. Box 277, Mount Rainier, MD 20712.

But if your primary interest is finding out where UFOs are being seen *right now*, your best bet is to subscribe to an Internet UFO newsletter like *Filer's Files*, a weekly with current reports and other material. Produced by George A. Filer, the Eastern Director for the Mutual UFO Network, the newsletter is available from him at *Majorstar@aol.com*. Also available again is *UFO Roundup* by Joseph Trainor. Back issues and subscription information can be found at *http://ufoinfo.com/roundup*. If you need daily updates on UFO and related matters, try Canadian Errol Bruce-Knapp's *UFO Updates* at *updates@globalserve.net*.

A well-written, up-to-date, and always entertaining—but not free—web-based UFO newsletter is *CNI News* by Michael Lindemann. This biweekly newsletter runs about twenty-four pages and is available for $24 a year from *CNINews1@aol.com*.

And while you're on the web, check out our publication, *The Anomalist*, a semiannual journal with a web presence that explores the mysteries of science, history, and nature—including UFOs. Find us at *http://www.anomalist.com*.

CASE INDEX
(by date)

April 16, 1966	*Portage County, Ohio*	*114*
October 10, 1966	*Newton, Illinois*	*76*
November 22, 1966	*New York, New York*	*104*
October 26, 1967	*Moinge Downs, Dorset, England*	*124*
November 2, 1968	*Southeastern France*	*126*
January 1970	*Tronstad, Norway*	*64*
October 18, 1973	*Mansfield, Ohio*	*90*
October 25, 1973	*North West Cape, Western Australia*	*32*
January 12, 1975	*North Bergen, New Jersey*	*46*
October 28, 1975	*Loring Air Force Base, Maine*	*68*
July 1, 1977	*Aviano, Italy*	*116*
January 1978	*Cononley, Yorkshire, England*	*56*
January 27, 1978	*Frodsham, Cheshire, England*	*30*
May 10, 1978	*Emilcin, Poland*	*100*
December 29, 1980	*Huffman, Texas*	*112*
1982	*Central Valley, California*	*130*
June 1984	*Mediterranean Sea*	*50*
July 24, 1984	*Buchanan, New York*	*120*
November 17, 1986	*Fort Yukon, Alaska*	*98*
January 20, 1988	*Mundrabilla, Australia*	*80*
July 7, 1989	*Kanazawa, Japan*	*34*
July 28, 1989	*Kapustin Yar, Astrakhan, Russia*	*58*
March 14, 1995	*St. Petersburg, Russia*	*118*
May 25, 1995	*Bovina, Texas*	*86*
September 29, 1995	*Vejle, Jutland, Denmark*	*62*
October 5, 1996	*Pelotas, Brazil*	*110*